Just
LIKE MOTHER
USED TO MAKE

Food from the '30s and '40s

Compiled by Angela Nilsen and June Weatherall

Designed by Ian Escott
Photographs by Studio Lorenzini
Hand-colouring by Michael Barton
Published by Circle Books

First published in 1980 by Circle Books, Elm
House, Elm Street, London WC1X 0BP

We would like to thank 'Home and Country'
magazine for permission to use the drawings
on pages 27, 67 and 93: The Stork Cookery
Service for those on pages 44 and 108: Faber &
Faber for those by Joy Batchelor on pages 28
and 78 from 'Food Without Fuss': Gerald
Duckworth & Co for the Heath Robinson cartoon on page 26.

Heath Robinson cartoon © estate of Mrs J. C.
Heath Robinson, 1973.

Filmset and printed by W & J Mackay Limited,
Chatham, Kent

ISBN 0 907120 02 4

CONTENTS

CONTENTS

CONTENTS

METRICATION

oz/fluid oz	approx. g and ml	recommended conversion
1	28	25
2	57	50
3	85	75
4	113	100
5 ($\frac{1}{4}$ pint)	142	150
6	170	175
7	198	200
8 ($\frac{1}{4}$ lb)	226	225
9	255	250
10 ($\frac{1}{2}$ pint)	283	275
11	311	300
12	340	350
13	368	375
14	396	400
15 ($\frac{3}{4}$ pint)	428	425
16 (1 lb)	456	450
17	484	475
18	512	500
19	541	550
20 (1 pint)	569	575

Thanks to these people, without whom this
book would never have happened

Ruth and Ken Carigan

Dorothy Badley

Dorothy Pike

Mrs Taylor

Mrs Spicer

Mr Cramp

Aunty Louisa, Hannah, Emily, Ellen

You Give HALF A CUP OF MILK WHEN YOU GIVE A 2d BAR

Cadbury's

Nostalgia was the first inspiration for this book – 'do you remember that steamed treacle pudding your mother used to make?' . . . 'my grandmother did a cake with grated carrot in it'.

We began researching, talking to the women who were cooking for their families at that period – when money and food were scarce – discussing ingredients with them, noting down the recipes they remembered.

It was then it began to strike us that here was more than nostalgia – a way of thinking and dealing with food and feeding a family and friends that are very relevant today. The feeling of belt-tightening, coping, making the best of things.

But circumstances and people's taste are not quite the same now as they were in the 1930s and 40s. We don't have dried eggs and no one would actually be happy eating the cardboard-consistency pastry recommended by Lord Woolton for his famous pie, so we have adapted the recipes slightly, when we tested them, to make them acceptable to the cooks and families of today.

But the nostalgia hasn't disappeared, why should it? We've tried to make this book look right. The photographs aren't the lavish, glossy ones of present day cookbooks, but were taken in black and white and then coloured by the almost forgotten art of colour spraying – remember those seaside scenes on postcards? And the advertisements – we feel sure that they'll revive dim and distant memories.

We hope you'll enjoy this visual trip down memory lane, but don't forget this is a practical cookery book, full of recipes for good, nourishing, comforting food – just like mother used to make.

SAVE FUEL

Keep warm inside

with

CROSSE & BLACKWELL'S

SOUPS

Soups that Nourish

Unexcelled since 1706 for Quality

CROSSE & BLACKWELL'S

Satisfying Soups

The warm, appetizing smell coming from a steaming bowl of soup – what could be a better way of saying 'welcome home' to a hungry family or friends either at lunchtime or in the evening.

Soups are the cook's friend – served at the start they can make a skimpy, otherwise uninteresting meal seem more than it actually is – or a thick, nourishing broth can be a complete meal in itself. The recipes on the following pages are for satisfying family soups – they don't use exotic or expensive ingredients – but simple everyday and inexpensive meats, vegetables and pulses.

The cook of the 1930s and 40s probably had a stockpot perpetually bubbling away on the range – today few of us have ranges, but we do have stock cubes! We also have pressure cookers to speed up the soup-making process and liquidisers to save us rubbing things through sieves.

Yes, times change, but the appeal and quality of the steaming bowl of soup still, thankfully, remains.

HODGE PODGE

Serves 4

The dried peas or beans used in this meal-in-itself soup have to be soaked overnight.

4 oz dried peas or beans
¾ lb shin of beef or middle neck of lamb
1 lb potatoes
1 medium-sized onion
2 carrots
1½ pints beef stock
Salt and pepper
Dumplings:
4 oz self-raising flour
2 oz shredded suet
½ level teaspoon salt
½ teaspoon dried sage

Soak the peas or beans in water overnight, then strain and rinse in cold water.

Trim off the excess fat from the meat and cut the meat into mouth-sized pieces. Peel the potatoes and cut into large pieces; peel and chop the onion, peel and thickly slice the carrots. Place all the ingredients, with the stock and salt and pepper, in a large saucepan. Cover with a lid and bring to the boil. Simmer gently for about 1½ to 2 hours, or until the beans and meat are almost tender.

To make the dumplings, place the flour in a mixing bowl with the remaining ingredients. Add 3 to 4 tablespoons of water to mix to a soft but not sticky dough. Form the dough into small dumplings; drop them into the soup, cover the saucepan and continue cooking for a further 20 minutes.

VEGETABLE BROTH

Serves 6

Except for nutmeg and cheese, most of us have got out of the grating habit these days. So although this recipe calls for grated carrot, parsnip, and potato, chopping them very finely would do just as well. Use a medium-sized example of each vegetable. Serve with small squares of toasted bread.

1 carrot
1 parsnip
1 onion
1 potato
2 or 3 celery stalks
1 leek
1½ oz butter
Salt and pepper
Chicken stock

Peel the carrot, parsnip, onion and potato. Wash and trim the celery and the leek. Grate the carrot, parsnip, onion and potato and chop the leek and celery stalks finely.

Melt the butter over a low heat, then add the prepared carrot, parsnip, onion, potato and leek. Cover the saucepan with a lid and, shaking frequently, cook over a low heat until the onion is clear.

Add the chopped celery, season, and cover with stock. Simmer for 25 to 35 minutes.

Pour the broth into a hot tureen and hand diced toasted bread separately.

KIDNEY SOUP

Serves 4

⅓ lb kidney
1 medium-sized onion
1 oz margarine
2 pints beef stock
1 large carrot
¼ lb turnip
1 tablespoon tomato ketchup
Salt and pepper
Sprig of parsley
1 heaped tablespoon flour

Wash the kidneys, remove the skin and core. Peel and slice the onion. Melt the margarine in a saucepan and fry the kidney and onion to a rich brown colour, then chop the kidney. Return to the saucepan. Add the stock.

Peel and slice the carrot, peel and cut the turnip into cubes; add with the tomato ketchup, salt, pepper and parsley, to the saucepan. Bring to boiling point, skim, cover

and simmer for about 1¼ hours skimming again if necessary.

Blend the flour with a little cold water and add to the soup, stirring continuously until thickened. Boil for 5 minutes.

PEA POD SOUP

Serves 4

When you are cooking fresh peas, don't throw away the pods. Turn them into this unusual soup.

1 lb pea pods
½ lb potatoes
1 oz margarine
2 pints chicken stock
4 sprigs fresh mint or 1 teaspoon dried mint
Salt and pepper
1 oz cornflour
¼ pint milk
1 tablespoon chopped parsley
1 teaspoon sugar

Wash the pea pods thoroughly and remove the stalks and tough stringy threads. Peel the potatoes and chop into small cubes. Melt the margarine in a saucepan and fry the potatoes lightly. Pour in the chicken stock; add the pea pods, mint and salt and pepper to taste. Cook until the pods are tender. Rub through a sieve and return the soup to the saucepan.

Blend the cornflour with the milk, stir into the soup and bring to the boil, stirring, until thickened and smooth. Cook for 2 minutes and stir in the chopped parsley and sugar just before serving.

GOLDEN SOUP

Serves 4 to 6

1½ lb carrots
1 small onion
1½ pints chicken stock
Salt and pepper
½ teaspoon dried thyme
½ pint milk

Peel and slice the carrots, peel and chop the onion. Place in a saucepan with the stock, salt and pepper and thyme and simmer until tender, about 40 minutes.

Rub the soup through a sieve, or liquidise. Return the soup to the saucepan, stir in the milk and reheat.

CARROT SOUP

Serves 4 to 6

A rasher of bacon gives this soup a delicious flavour.

1 lb carrots
1 medium-sized onion
1 stick of celery
1 rasher of bacon
1 oz margarine or dripping
2 pints chicken stock
Salt and pepper
1 oz cornflour
½ pint milk
Chopped parsley

Peel the carrots and then grate them coarsely. Peel and chop the onion; wash and chop the celery. Remove the rind from the bacon and chop the bacon. Place in a saucepan with the margarine or dripping. Fry gently for about 5 minutes without browning. Add the stock and the seasoning, cover and simmer gently for about ¾ hour. Rub through a sieve or liquidise.

Mix the cornflour smoothly with the milk, add to the soup and bring to the boil, stirring, until thickened. Boil gently for 3 minutes before serving. Serve sprinkled with chopped parsley.

LENTIL SOUP

Serves 4

5 oz red lentils
1 medium-sized carrot, turnip and onion
2 sticks celery
2 oz margarine
2 pints chicken stock
Salt and pepper
1 teaspoon mixed dried herbs
1 bay leaf
Freshly chopped parsley to garnish

Wash and drain the lentils.

Peel and slice the carrot; peel and chop the turnip and onion; wash and slice the celery.

Melt the margarine in a large saucepan, add the vegetables and fry gently for 5 minutes. Add the drained lentils, the stock, seasoning and herbs. Bring the soup to the boil, then simmer gently, uncovered, until all the vegetables are soft and the soup is thickened, about 40 minutes.

Remove the bay leaf. Serve the soup sprinkled with chopped parsley.

Sailor's Pie, page 29

Bubble and Squeak, page 30

Spring Greens and Bacon
with Egg Sauce, page 43

Fish Envelope, page 49

Cold Beef Loaf with Horseradish, page 35

Stuffed Onions with Beef
and Mushroom Filling, page 41

Cottage Pie Crumble, page 35

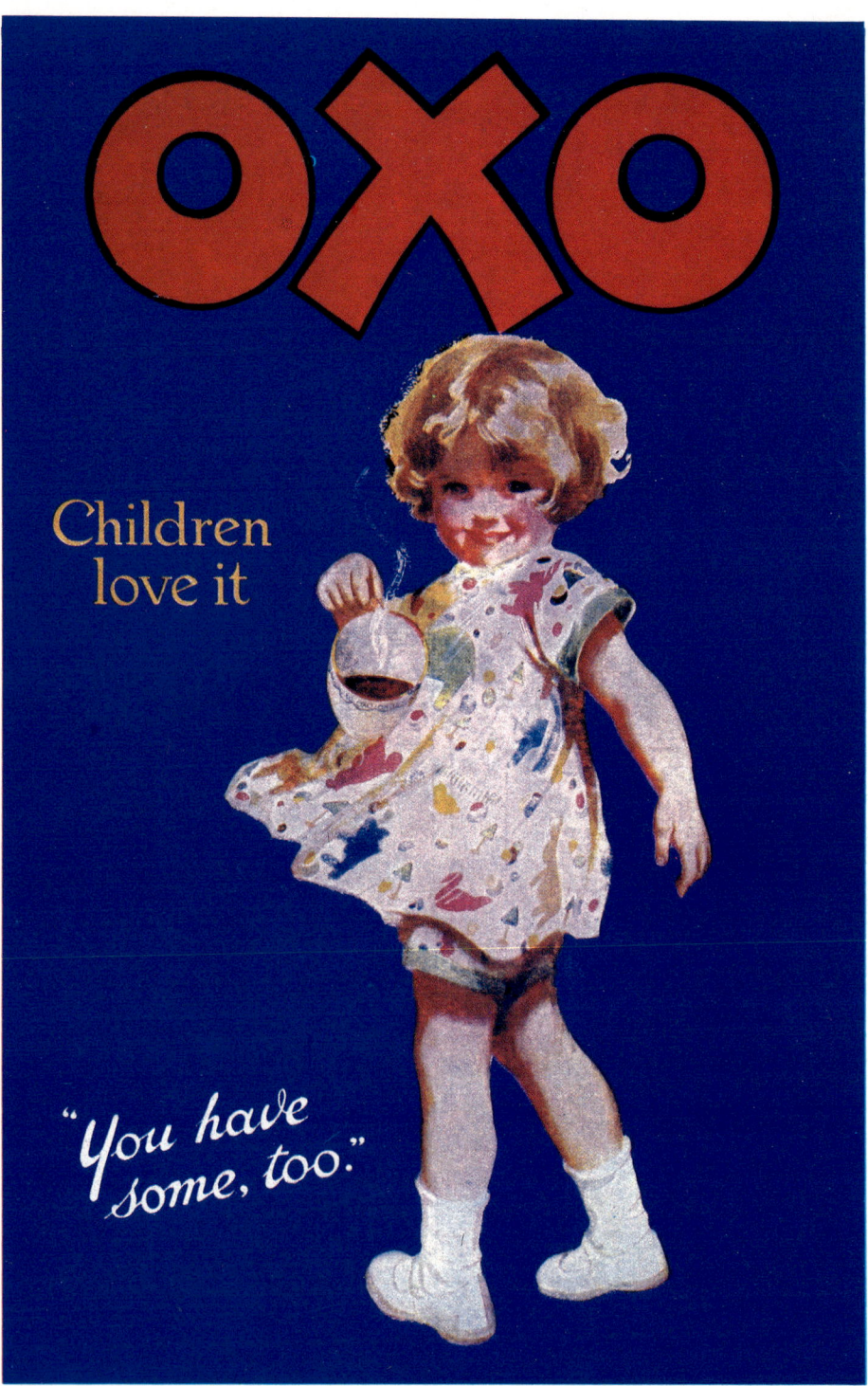

TOMATO SOUP

Serves 4

1 medium-sized potato
1 medium-sized carrot
1 stick celery
1 oz margarine
1½ pints chicken stock
1 (12 oz) tin tomatoes
Salt and pepper

Peel and cut the potato into cubes; peel and slice the carrot and wash and slice the celery. Melt the margarine in a saucepan and fry the potato, carrot and celery lightly without browning. Pour in the stock and bring to the boil.

Stir in the contents of the tin of tomatoes and season to taste with salt and pepper. Simmer, uncovered, about 40 minutes until the vegetables are tender and then rub through a sieve or liquidise.

Return the soup to the saucepan and reheat.

BEETROOT SOUP

Serves 4

This soup is a beautiful colour.

1 lb raw beetroot
1 medium-sized potato
1 onion
1 oz margarine
2½ pints chicken stock
Salt and pepper
Pinch grated nutmeg
Double cream (optional)

Peel the beetroot and potato and cut into cubes. Peel and chop the onion.

Melt the margarine in a saucepan and lightly fry the vegetables. Stir in the stock and salt and pepper. Bring to the boil, then turn down the heat and simmer for about 1 hour.

Rub the soup through a sieve or liquidise. Return the soup to the saucepan and heat again thoroughly. Stir in the nutmeg, check the seasoning, and serve topped with a little cream if wished.

BRUSSELS SPROUT SOUP

Serves 4

A lovely green soup you can serve with thin slices of toast.

2 rashers streaky bacon
1 medium-sized onion
1 oz margarine
¼ lb Brussels sprouts
Salt and pepper
1 pint chicken stock
Milk
Green colouring (optional)
Crisply fried bacon pieces

Remove the rind from the bacon and cut the bacon into small pieces. Peel and chop the onion. Melt the margarine in a saucepan, and fry the bacon and onion.

Take off any damaged outside leaves from the sprouts, slice each sprout in half and add to the saucepan with the cooked bacon, salt and pepper and stock. Cover and simmer for about 25 minutes, or until the sprouts are tender.

Rub the soup through a sieve, or liquidise.

Add some milk, if necessary to thin the soup down and a little green colouring to improve the colour if wished, and warm through. Serve sprinkled with crisply fried bacon pieces.

LEEK AND POTATO SOUP

Serves 4 to 6

A few tablespoons of cream can be stirred into this soup just before serving to make it really creamy.

1 lb leeks
1 onion
1 lb potatoes
1½ oz margarine
Salt and pepper
2 pints of chicken stock

Wash the leeks thoroughly and cut them into small pieces, using as much of the green as possible and only discarding the toughest looking parts. Peel and chop the onion. Peel and cut the potatoes into cubes.

Melt the margarine in a large saucepan, and lightly fry the vegetables, without browning them. Stir in the salt and pepper and stock. Bring to the boil, then turn down the heat and simmer for about 40 minutes or until the vegetables are cooked.

Rub the soup through a sieve or liquidise. Return to the saucepan and heat again thoroughly. Check the seasoning and then serve.

DRIED GREEN PEA SOUP

Serves 6

This soup needs thinking about the day before, for the dried peas need soaking overnight. If you like thinner soups have some warm water, stock or milk ready, to achieve the desired consistency before serving.

½ lb dried green split peas
2½ pints chicken stock
2 medium-sized onions
1 carrot
2 sticks of celery
½ teaspoon dried mint
Salt
Black pepper
1 oz margarine

Soak the peas overnight in enough cold water to cover them. The following day drain them in a sieve and rinse in fresh cold water.

Place the stock in a saucepan and heat until it is warm. Peel the onions and carrot, wash the celery and chop them all fairly finely. Add the drained peas, the onion, celery, dried mint and seasoning to the warm water. Bring to the boil and boil for 5 minutes. Then simmer until the dried peas can be squashed between the fingers, about 1 to 1½ hours.

Rub through a sieve or liquidise, and return the soup to the saucepan over a low heat. Cut the margarine into small pieces and add to the soup, stirring until it is melted.

TO PUT THE FLAVOUR INTO
THAT STEW USE . . .

FOSTER CLARK'S SOUPS

CABBAGE SOUP WITH DUMPLINGS

Serves 6

You can turn this into a main meal by adding thinly sliced cooked sausages (smoked ones like frankfurters give the best flavour). Just simmer the slices in the soup when the dumplings are added.

1 small cabbage
3 rashers streaky bacon
1 small onion
1 oz margarine
2 pints chicken stock
Pinch of grated nutmeg
Salt and pepper
Dumplings:
4 oz self-raising flour
2 oz margarine or shredded suet
½ level teaspoon salt
½ teaspoon mixed dried herbs

Remove the outer leaves from the cabbage; remove the rind from the bacon, chop the bacon then slice the cabbage finely. Peel and chop the onion. Melt the margarine in a large saucepan and fry the onion and bacon lightly. Add the cabbage and toss in the hot fat for a minute or two. Add the stock, nutmeg, and salt and pepper to taste, bring to the boil, then cover and simmer for 15 minutes.

Meanwhile make the dumplings. Place the flour in a mixing bowl; rub in the margarine until the mixture resembles fine breadcrumbs, or stir in the suet; add the salt and mixed herbs. Add sufficient water to mix to a soft but not sticky dough. Form the dough into small dumplings and drop them into the soup. Cover and continue cooking for a further 20 minutes. Serve at once.

Smoked Haddock Soup

1 medium size onion
3 rashers streaky bacon
2½ oz margarine
1 large potato
1½ oz flour
3/4 pint milk
3/4 lb smoked haddock
Salt and pepper
1 tablespoon fresh chopped parsley

Peel and chop onion. Remove rind from bacon & chop bacon. Melt 1oz of the marge in a saucepan & fry onion and bacon until the onion is soft. Peel & cut potato into cubes, add to the saucepan & cook gently until potato is cooked, stir occasionally. Melt remaining marge in another saucepan, stir in flour, cook ½ minute. Remove from heat add milk gradually. Return to heat bring to boil, stir until thick & smooth. Mix in onion & potato. Skin Haddock cut into bite size pieces. Place in sauce, simmer gently 10 mins or until fish is cooked. Season to taste with salt & pepper & stir in chopped parsley. Soup can be thinned down with extra milk.

OXTAIL SOUP

Serves 6

This is splendid for cold nights. It is a soup well worth taking trouble over and should be served piping hot.

1 oxtail
2 medium-sized onions
1 carrot
1 small turnip
2 leeks
1½ oz margarine
3 pints beef stock or water
Blade of mace
3 cloves
6 peppercorns
1 bay leaf
Sprig of fresh parsley or thyme
Salt
1 oz flour
2 teaspoons Worcestershire sauce

Wash the oxtail and cut it into joints. Peel and slice the vegetables. Melt the margarine in a saucepan and fry the meat and vegetables until evenly browned.

Add 3 pints of beef stock or water, the spices, peppercorns, herbs and salt. Cover and simmer very slowly for about 3½ hours, or until the meat is tender. Strain into a bowl (removing the oxtail and cutting the meat from the bone; reserve the meat) and leave until quite cold, preferably overnight. This step in the work is important, for it enables all the fat to be removed from the surface.

After the fat has been skimmed from the surface of the cooled oxtail liquid, blend a little of the liquid with the flour in a saucepan. Stir in the remaining liquid, and bring to the boil, stirring, until thickened. Return the meat to the soup with the Worcestershire sauce, and taste to check the seasoning. Simmer for 5 minutes before serving.

FISH SOUP

Serves 4

You can use any variety of fish for this soup.

1 lb white fish
1 onion
1 carrot
Stick of celery
Blade of mace
4 peppercorns
1 clove
1 bay leaf
Sprig of parsley
1½ oz butter or margarine
1½ oz flour
½ pint milk

Remove the skin and bones from the fish and cut the fish into pieces. Peel and slice the onion and carrot; wash and slice the celery. Place the vegetables in a saucepan with the mace, peppercorns, clove, bay leaf, parsley and 1½ pints of water. Bring to boiling point and simmer for 15 minutes. Add the pieces of fish and simmer for a further 15 minutes. Strain and reserve 1 pint of the liquid.

Melt the butter or margarine in a saucepan, stir in the flour and cook for half a minute. Remove from the heat and add the milk gradually with the strained liquid. Return to the heat and cook, stirring, until thickened and smooth. Add the pieces of the cooked fish to the soup with the vegetables. Warm the soup through very gently.

RATIONAL GADGETS FOR YOUR COUPONS.
DOUBLING GLOUCESTER CHEESES BY THE GRUYÈRE
METHOD.

DRAWN BY W. HEATH ROBINSON.

Appetising Main Meals

When meat and fish are cheap and plentiful cooks get lazy – steak, fillets of fish or chops are popped under the grill or fried, and that's that. But in the 30s and 40s these raw ingredients were expensive and, during wartime, scarce and so the British family cook of the time had to be an inventive caterer – supplying her family with both nutritious and interesting main meals, making a little go a long way.

Of course cheaper cuts of meat and fish require more time-consuming cooking and preparing, but to most cooks the time spent is amply rewarded by the pleased reaction of their families and friends to simple, honest, tasty food. The recipes that follow are for meat and fish meals, ingenious concoctions from leftovers and egg, cheese and vegetable supper dishes.

MINCED BEEF ROLY POLY

Serves 4

½ lb minced beef
½ lb sausagemeat
1 tablespoon chopped parsley
2 teaspoons made mustard
Salt and pepper
8 oz suet pastry (see page 65)

Grease a large sheet of double greaseproof paper.

Mix together the minced beef, sausagemeat, parsley, mustard, salt and pepper.

Roll out the pastry to an 8 inch square. Spread the meat mixture to within 1 inch of the edges of the pastry. Damp the edges of the pastry with a little water, roll up loosely and seal the ends well together.

Wrap up loosely in the greased greaseproof, sealing the ends well.

Place in a steamer over boiling water and steam for 2 hours. Carefully remove from the steamer, unwrap and serve with Spiced Tomato Sauce (see page 44).

BEEF AND MUSHROOM PIE

Serves 4

2 level tablespoons flour
1 teaspoon salt
½ teaspoon pepper
1 lb stewing steak
½ lb kidney
1 medium-sized onion
¼ lb mushrooms
1 (7½ oz) packet frozen flaky or puff pastry, thawed
Milk

In a basin mix together the 2 tablespoons flour and the salt and pepper. Trim the meat and cut into mouth-sized pieces. Prepare the kidney by removing the skin and cores and cutting into pieces. Peel and slice the onion. Roll the stewing steak and kidney in the seasoned flour. Place the meat and the onion into a saucepan with enough water to cover. Bring to the boil, stirring, and then simmer for about 1½ hours, or until the meat is tender. Allow to cool.

Preheat the oven to 425°F, Gas Mark 7. Place the meat in a 1½ pint pie dish with the mushrooms. Pour in enough of the meat liquid to just cover the meat mixture.

Roll out the pastry a little bit larger than the top of the dish on a lightly floured surface. Put a thin strip of pastry on to the dampened rim of the pie dish, moisten it, and cover the top with the pastry lid, making a small hole in the top for the steam to escape. Trim off the surplus pastry, seal the edges. Decorate the top of the pie with pastry 'leaves' made from the pastry trimmings. Brush the pastry with milk.

Bake for 15 minutes, then reduce the temperature to 350°F, Gas Mark 4 for a further 15 to 20 minutes or until the pastry is risen and golden.

SAILORS' PIE

Serves 4

In this recipe a pastry crust is added to the saucepan containing the other ingredients. It then cooks in the steam.

2 tablespoons flour
1 teaspoon salt
½ teaspoon pepper
1½ lb stewing steak
2 oz margarine
2 medium-sized onions
½ lb carrots
1 (8 oz) tin tomatoes
¾ pint beef stock
1 bay leaf
3 cloves
Salt and pepper
For the crust:
6 oz self-raisng flour
¼ level teaspoon salt
3 oz margarine

In a basin mix together the 2 tablespoons of flour and the salt and pepper.

Trim the meat and cut into mouth-sized pieces and roll in the seasoned flour. Melt the margarine in a large saucepan and fry the meat until it is browned. Peel and chop the onions and add to the browned meat; fry them lightly. Peel and cut the carrots into lengthways strips. Add the tomatoes and carrots to the saucepan. Pour in the stock, add the bay leaf and cloves; season with salt and pepper.

Bring slowly to the boil then simmer covered, on a low heat for 1 hour. Meanwhile make the crust by mixing the flour and salt together and then rubbing in the margarine, until the mixture resembles fine breadcrumbs. Mix in sufficient water to make a stiff dough.

Knead gently until smooth on a lightly floured surface and roll into a round of ½ inch thickness, and the size in diameter of the top of the saucepan. Remove the saucepan from the heat. Place the crust into the saucepan over the meat, and simmer slowly for a further 45 minutes to 1 hour.

LIVER AND BACON HOT-POT

Serves 4

As this is a slow cooking casserole dish, you can use the cheaper types of liver.

¾ lb liver
1 tablespoon flour
½ teaspoon salt
¼ teaspoon pepper
1 teaspoon dried rosemary
¼ lb streaky bacon
1 large onion
1½ lb potatoes
Beef stock

Preheat the oven to 325°F, Gas Mark 3.

Wash the liver and cut it into pieces about 2 inches long. Mix together the flour, salt, pepper and rosemary and roll the pieces of liver in it. Remove the rind from the bacon and chop the bacon. Peel and slice the onion and peel and slice the potatoes fairly thinly.

Arrange the liver, bacon, onion and potatoes in layers in a casserole dish, finishing with a layer of potatoes. Add sufficient stock to come three quarters of the way up the casserole. Cover and bake for 1½ to 2 hours, removing the cover for the last 20 minutes of the cooking time, to brown the potato.

CORNED BEEF HASH

Serves 4

1 large onion
2 carrots
2 large potatoes
1 oz margarine
⅓ oz flour
½ pint beef stock
Salt and pepper
1 (12 oz) tin corned beef

Peel and slice the onion and the carrots. Peel and chop the potatoes into cubes. Melt the margarine in a large frying pan then add the onion and carrot and potatoes and fry until lightly browned. Stir in the flour and continue frying until this is brown, stirring all the time to prevent burning.

Add the stock gradually, stirring until thickened and smooth, then simmer a few minutes until the vegetables are tender. Season with salt and pepper.

Cut the corned beef into neat pieces and, a few minutes before serving, add it to the saucepan to heat through.

BUBBLE AND SQUEAK

A traditionally delicious way of using leftover boiled beef, potatoes and greens of any kind. It's useful to have two frying pans for this dish. If you haven't, cook the meat first and keep it warm.

Leftover cooked beef
Leftover mashed cooked potato
Leftover cooked chopped cabbage or greens
Salt and black pepper
Fat for frying

The cooked beef is cut into slices and fried on both sides. Mix the potatoes and cooked cabbage or greens and season with salt and black pepper. Fry this mixture in another frying pan, turning once until well cooked and browned on both sides, and serve with the fried beef slices.

ONION AND BACON TART

Serves 4

4 oz shortcrust pastry (see page 65)
4 medium-sized onions
2½ oz margarine
4 rashers streaky bacon
1½ oz flour
⅓ pint milk
Salt and pepper
2 oz cheese, grated

Roll out the pastry on a lightly floured surface and use it to line an 8 inch shallow cake tin or pie dish. Bake the pastry 'blind'.

Peel and finely chop the onions; melt 2 oz of the margarine in a saucepan and fry the onions until soft. Remove the rind from the bacon, grill the bacon and when cooked, cut into small pieces. Stir the flour and the remaining ½ oz of margarine into the saucepan with the onions until all are well blended. Remove from the heat and stir in the milk gradually. Bring to the boil, stirring, until thickened and smooth.

Remove from the heat, stir in the bacon and salt and pepper and pour into the pastry lined tin or pie dish. Sprinkle over the grated cheese, and grill until the cheese is golden brown.

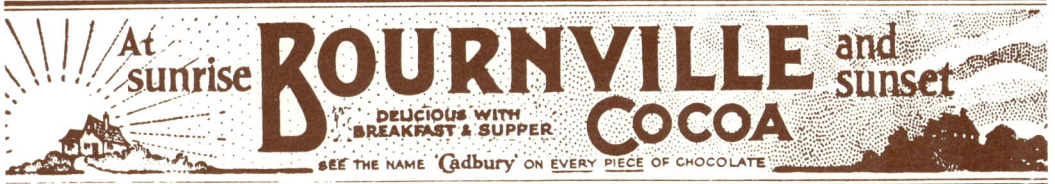

PORK AND APPLE CASSEROLE

Serves 4

For this succulent dish use cheaper cuts of pork.

1½ lb pork spare rib
1 large onion
2 large cooking apples
Salt and pepper
1 teaspoon dried sage
Chicken stock
4 large potatoes

Preheat the oven to 325°F, Gas Mark 3.

Trim off the excess fat from the pork and cut the pork into neat pieces. Peel and slice the onion thinly. Peel, core and slice the apples.

Arrange the prepared ingredients in layers in a large ovenproof dish, season with salt and pepper and sprinkle over the sage. Pour in enough stock to almost cover the meat.

Peel and slice the potatoes and arrange neatly all over the top. Cover and bake for 2 hours, removing the cover for about the last 20 minutes of the cooking time, to brown the potato.

KIDNEY, BACON AND SAUSAGE FRY WITH LEEK SAUCE

Serves 4

1½ lb leeks
4 kidneys
4 rashers bacon
4 sausages
1 oz margarine
Salt and pepper

Trim the leeks, wash and slice them. Cook in boiling salted water until tender, drain well, reserving the liquid. Rub the leeks through a sieve or liquidise.

Prepare the kidneys by removing the skin and core, and cut them into small pieces. Remove the rind from the bacon and chop the bacon. Slice each sausage into four. Melt the margarine in a saucepan and fry the bacon until crisp. Remove, and fry the kidneys and sausages until brown. Add the bacon, ¼ pint of the reserved leek liquid, salt and pepper.

Cover the pan and simmer very gently for 15 minutes, stirring frequently. Stir in the leek pulp and simmer gently for about a further 30 minutes, or until the kidney is tender.

TOAD IN THE HOLE

Serves 4

The addition of the chopped onion make this traditional dish extra tasty.

1 lb sausages
1 oz lard
4 oz plain flour
½ teaspoon salt
1 egg
½ pint milk and water
1 small onion

Preheat the oven to 425°F, Gas Mark 7.

Place the sausages in a shallow baking tin with the lard. Place in the preheated oven and cook for 15 minutes. Meanwhile prepare the batter, place the flour and salt into a mixing bowl. Make a well in the centre, add the egg and half of the milk and water. Beat well until smooth; then beat in the remaining milk and water gradually. Peel and chop the onion finely and add to the batter.

After 15 minutes remove the sausages from the oven and pour over the batter. Replace in the oven and cook for about 45 minutes, or until the batter is well risen and golden.

PLOUGHMAN'S PIE

Serves 4

For the vegetable stock use the water the vegetables have been cooked in.

¾ lb cold meat (beef or chicken)
1 teaspoon curry powder
¼ teaspoon grated nutmeg
1 large onion
1 oz margarine
1 large carrot
2 tablespoons freshly chopped parsley
Salt and pepper
Vegetable or chicken stock
6 oz shortcrust pastry (see page 65)

Remove any fat or gristle from the meat and chop it roughly. Put it into a basin and mix it with the curry powder and nutmeg. Peel and chop the onion; melt the margarine and fry the onion until soft. Peel and grate the carrot. Mix the onion and carrot with the meat, parsley, salt and pepper and a little stock to make the mixture quite moist (it should be like thick porridge). Preheat the oven to 400°F, Gas Mark 6.

Place the meat mixture into a shallow pie dish. Roll out the pastry a little bit larger than the top of the dish on a lightly floured surface. Put a thin strip of pastry on to the dampened rim of the pie dish, moisten it and cover the top with the pastry lid, making a small hole in the top for the steam to escape. Trim off the surplus pastry and seal the edges. Bake in the preheated oven for 30 minutes or until the pastry is golden brown.

CORNED BEEF AND VEGETABLE PIE

Serves 4 to 5

2 lb potatoes
1 leek
1 oz margarine
Milk
Salt and pepper
½ lb carrots
1 onion
1 heart of small cabbage
8 oz corned beef
1 level tablespoon flour
1 level tablespoon gravy powder
1 to 2 oz cheese, grated

Peel the potatoes and cut into halves, wash, trim and chop the leek. Boil the potatoes until tender, adding the chopped leek for the last 10 minutes of cooking time. Remove four halves of the potatoes and put to one side; drain the remainder. Mash the leek and potatoes with the margarine and a little milk and season well.

Peel and slice the carrots and onion. Cook in a saucepan with enough water to cover. Meanwhile shred the cabbage heart and add to the boiling water 10 minutes after the carrots and onion. When these vegetables are tender, drain them, reserving the liquid. Preheat the oven to 375°F, Gas Mark 5.

Dice the corned beef and the four halves of potatoes and mix them well with the drained vegetables. Put them all into a big pie dish, and season with salt and pepper.

Measure ¾ pint of the vegetable cooking liquid (add water to make up if necessary). Blend into the flour and gravy powder in a saucepan and bring to the boil, stirring, until thickened and smooth. Add about three quarters to the meat and vegetable mixture. Cover the top of the pie dish with the mashed potato and leek and spread over with a fork. Bake in the preheated oven for 20 minutes, then remove from the oven and sprinkle the top with the grated cheese, replace in the oven and cook for another 15 minutes. Serve with the remaining gravy.

MEAT AND BATTER PUDDING

Serves 4

4 oz plain flour
½ teaspoon salt
1 egg
½ pint milk and water
1 onion
1 oz margarine
¾ lb minced beef
½ teaspoon mixed dried herbs
Salt and pepper
1 tablespoon tomato ketchup

Preheat the oven to 425°F, Gas Mark 7. Grease a shallow ovenproof dish, or baking tin.

To make the batter place the flour and the salt in a mixing bowl, make a well in the centre, add the egg and half of the milk and water. Beat well until smooth, then beat in the remaining milk and water gradually.

Peel and chop the onion. Melt the margarine and fry the onion lightly, add the meat and cook for 15 minutes. Mix in the herbs, salt and pepper and tomato ketchup. Place in the bottom of the pie dish. Pour the batter over the meat and bake for about 45 minutes, or until the batter is well risen and golden.

Cornish Pasties - enough for 4

Ingredients - Cold minced or chopped leftover meat,
or fresh mince

1- small onion   .1- large potato
½ lb - meat   1- teas. chopped parsley
Salt & pepper   1- Egg
8oz Shortcrust Pastry

Method

Peel & chop onion finely. Peel & cut potato
into small dice. Put meat, parsley, onion
and potato into bowl, season and add
2 Tabs water. Mix well.
Preheat oven 400°F or Gas Mark 6
Divide pastry into 4 and roll each
into a circle. Beat egg, brush edges
of pastry circles.
Divide meat mix into 4 and place
each in middle of pastry circles.
Bring edges together, press well and flute
with fingers.
Brush all over each pasty with beaten
egg, place on baking tray and bake
for 15 mins. to brown pastry, reduce
heat to 325°F. Gas Mark 3. Cook for
further 45 mins. to 1 hour.
Serve hot or cold.

COTTAGE PIE CRUMBLE

Serves 4

1 medium-sized onion
2 medium-sized carrots
2 oz margarine
1 oz plain flour
½ pint milk
¼ lb fresh or frozen peas
1 (12 oz) tin corned beef
Salt and pepper
2 tomatoes
Topping:
2 oz margarine
4 oz self-raising flour
½ teaspoon salt
¼ teaspoon pepper
1 tablespoon freshly chopped parsley
2 oz Cheddar cheese

Grease a 2 pint pie dish.

Peel and chop the onion; peel and slice the carrots. Melt 1 oz of the margarine in a saucepan and lightly fry the vegetables. Remove the vegetables and melt the remaining 1 oz margarine in the pan. Blend in the flour, return to the heat and cook for half a minute. Remove from the heat and stir in the milk very gradually. Bring to the boil, stirring, until thickened and smooth. Place the onion and carrots in the sauce.

Add the peas to the sauce, and simmer for 5 minutes. Chop the corned beef and stir into the sauce, seasoning to taste with salt and pepper. Place the sauce mixture in the pie dish. Slice the tomatoes and arrange them on top of the sauce. Preheat the oven to 350°F, Gas Mark 4.

To make the topping, rub the margarine into the flour until the mixture resembles fine breadcrumbs. Stir in the remaining ingredients and sprinkle over the sauce. Bake for 35 to 45 minutes or until golden.

COLD BEEF LOAF WITH HORSERADISH

Serves 4

This meat loaf is equally delicious served hot with a good gravy.

1 medium-sized onion
4 oz bacon or ham
1¼ lb minced beef
1 oz fresh breadcrumbs
2 tablespoons freshly chopped parsley
½ teaspoon mixed herbs
¼ teaspoon mixed spice
¼ teaspoon nutmeg
Salt and pepper
1 egg, beaten
Horseradish sauce

Preheat oven to 350°F, Gas Mark 4. Grease a 1 lb loaf tin and line the bottom with greaseproof paper.

Peel and finely chop the onion; remove the rind from the bacon if used and finely chop or mince the bacon or ham. Place in a mixing bowl and mix with the remaining ingredients, except the horseradish sauce.

Pack the mixture in the prepared tin, cover with greased greaseproof paper and bake for 1 hour, or until the meat begins to shrink from the sides of the tin. Remove from the oven, and leave until the loaf is quite cold. Remove from the tin and spread a little horseradish sauce over the top.

SAVOURY PIE

Serves 4 to 5

8 oz wholewheat flour
Pinch of salt
2 oz margarine
2 oz cooking fat
¾ lb potatoes
2 medium-sized onions
¼ lb streaky bacon
2 tomatoes
4 oz cheese, grated
Freshly chopped or dried sage
Salt and pepper
2 tablespoons milk

Place the flour and salt in a mixing bowl. Rub in the margarine and cooking fat until the mixture resembles fine breadcrumbs. Mix in sufficient cold water and press lightly together to make a firm dough.

Roll out just over half the pastry on a lightly floured surface and use to line a 9 inch pie dish.

Peel then slice the potatoes very finely. Peel and chop the onions. Remove the rind from the bacon and chop the bacon into small squares. Slice the tomatoes. Preheat the oven to 375°F, Gas Mark 5.

Place half the sliced potatoes in the pastry case, then half the onions, followed by half the bacon and half the grated cheese. Sprinkle with a little sage. Repeat these layers once more and season with salt and pepper. Pour the milk over and then lay the sliced tomatoes on the top.

Roll out the remaining pastry to a circle for the lid. Damp the edge of the pastry and press on the lid, sealing the two edges firmly together. Decorate the edges by pressing lightly with a fork, and make a hole in the centre of the lid for the steam to escape.

Place in the preheated oven and bake for about 45 minutes, or until the pastry is a nice golden brown.

LORD WOOLTON PIE

Serves 4

Lord Woolton had the unenviable job of being Minister of Food during the Second World War. In our researches and testing, we found that the original recipe was a little dry, so we have adapted it slightly. Originally too, the pie was topped with a special fatless pie crust which we felt was a little austere for today's tastes, so we did add fat to the pastry.

1½ lb mixed root vegetables
4 spring onions
½ pint cheese sauce (see page 44)
2 tablespoons freshly chopped parsley
Salt and pepper
Pie crust:
6 oz wholewheat flour
Pinch of salt
1½ oz cooking fat
1½ oz margarine
½ teaspoon powdered sage

Peel the vegetables and cut into small dice. Cook them in boiling salted water until tender. Drain them well.

Trim and finely chop the onions and stir into the cheese sauce with the cooked vegetables, parsley and salt and pepper. Pour into a 1½ pint pie dish. Preheat the oven to 400°F, Gas Mark 6.

Pie crust: place the flour and salt in a mixing bowl. Rub in the cooking fat and margarine until the mixture resembles fine breadcrumbs.

36

Add the sage. Stir in sufficient cold water (about 2 tablespoons) to mix to a dough. Knead lightly on a lightly floured surface until smooth.

Roll out the pastry a little bit larger than the top of the dish. Put a thin strip of pastry on to the dampened rim of the pie dish, moisten it and cover the top with the pastry lid, making a small hole in the top for the steam to escape. Trim off the surplus pastry and seal the edges. Use the pastry trimmings to make pastry 'leaves' to decorate the pie.

Bake in the preheated oven for about 30 minutes or until the pastry is browned.

RABBIT HOT-POT

Serves 4

1 rabbit
½ lb onions or leeks
1 small swede
Salt and pepper
2 level tablespoons flour
2 tablespoons finely chopped parsley
Chicken stock
1 lb potatoes
1 rasher streaky bacon

Preheat the oven to 325°F, Gas Mark 3.

Wash the rabbit and cut into joints. Peel and slice the onions, if used, or wash and slice the leeks. Peel and dice the swede. Mix together the salt and pepper and flour and coat the rabbit joints in this. Place the vegetables and the rabbit joints in a large casserole, seasoning each layer, and sprinkling with the parsley.

Pour in sufficient stock to almost cover the rabbit.

Peel and slice the potatoes fairly thickly, and place in a layer on top. Remove the rind from the bacon. Chop the bacon and sprinkle over the potatoes. Sprinkle with salt and pepper, cover, and cook for 2 to 2½ hours, removing the lid for about the last 20 minutes of the cooking time, to brown the potatoes.

MINCE CAKES

Serves 4

2 rashers streaky bacon
1 small onion
1 oz margarine
4 oz cooked potatoes
1 egg
¾ lb minced beef
Salt and pepper
1 tablespoon freshly chopped parsley
½ teaspoon mixed dried herbs
2 teaspoons tomato ketchup
1 oz flour
Margarine for frying

Remove the rind from the bacon and chop the bacon very finely; peel and chop the onion very finely. Melt the margarine in a saucepan and lightly fry the bacon and onion.

Rub the potatoes through a sieve and mix into the fried bacon and onion. Beat the egg and stir in with the mince and the remaining ingredients, except the flour.

Form into small round cakes about ½ inch thick. Mix the flour with a little salt and pepper on a plate. Dip the mince cakes in the seasoned flour and coat thoroughly. Fry the mince cakes in melted margarine, turning, until golden brown. Serve with tomato sauce (see page 44).

SAVOURY KENTISH PUDDING

Serves 4

As this is a steamed pudding, have ready a large lidded saucepan with boiling water or a steamer.

8 oz suetcrust pastry (see page 65)
1 lb sausages
1 small onion
1 small apple
2 small tomatoes
1 tablespoon cornflour
Salt and pepper
1 teaspoon mixed herbs
3 tablespoons beef stock or water

Grease a 1½ pint pudding basin. Roll out three quarters of the pastry into a circle large enough to line the basin. Cut each sausage into 3 slices. Peel and slice the onion and apple, slice the tomatoes. Fill the basin with layers of these ingredients, sprinkling each layer with a little cornflour, seasoning and mixed herbs. Pour in the stock or water.

Roll out the remaining pastry to a circle for the lid, the same size as the top of the basin. Damp the edge of the pastry and press on the lid, sealing the two edges firmly together. Cover with greased greaseproof paper, or foil, and steam over boiling water for 2½ to 3 hours. Serve with Spiced Tomato Sauce (see page 44).

BRAISED HARICOT MINCE

Serves 4

Put the haricot beans to soak in water the day before you wish to cook this dish. Some frozen peas can be stirred into the haricot mince for the last five minutes of cooking time.

½ lb haricot beans
Salt
1 teaspoon powdered mustard
1 tablespoon Worcestershire sauce
3 carrots
1 onion
2 oz margarine
Pepper
¾ lb minced beef
1 level tablespoon gravy powder

Leave the haricot beans to soak in cold water overnight. The following day drain them in a sieve and rinse in cold water. Put them into fresh warm water (enough to well cover) in a saucepan with 1 teaspoon of salt, the mustard powder and the Worcestershire sauce. Simmer until almost tender, about 1½ hours. If you boil them too fast, the skins will come off.

Peel and slice the carrots and the onion. When the beans are almost tender, melt the margarine in a saucepan. Put in the sliced carrot and onion. Drain the beans, reserving the liquid, and add the beans to the carrot and onion. Season with salt and pepper, cover with a lid and cook for about 5 minutes.

Now add the meat and ½ pint of the bean liquid. Stir the contents of the saucepan with a fork to prevent the mince cooking in a lump. Simmer, covered, for about 20 minutes.

Blend another ¼ pint of the bean liquid (making up with water if necessary) with the gravy powder. Pour this into the saucepan and boil for about 5 minutes. Serve nice and hot with potatoes.

TRIPE AND ONIONS

Serves 4

Another way of cooking the tripe is to bake it in the oven until tender (about 3 hours at 300°F, Gas Mark 2) then use the liquid to make up the sauce as given below. Or, cook the tripe in a pressure cooker for 15 minutes.

1 lb tripe
1 lb onions
¾ pint milk
1 bay leaf
Salt and pepper
1 oz margarine
1 oz flour

Wash the tripe well, cover with cold water and bring slowly to the boil. Strain off the water and cut the tripe into strips. Peel and slice the onions and put them into a saucepan with the tripe, milk, ¼ pint of water, bay leaf, salt and pepper. Cover and simmer gently for 1½ to 2 hours, or until tender.

Strain off the stock and make up to 1 pint with water. Melt the margarine in a separate saucepan, stir in the flour and cook for half a minute. Remove from the heat and stir in the reserved stock gradually. Return the sauce to the heat and cook, stirring continuously until thickened and smooth. Return the tripe and onions to the sauce, reheat and serve as hot as possible with boiled potatoes.

STUFFED VEGETABLE MARROW

Serves 4

1 medium-sized marrow (about 2 to 2½ lb)
1 small onion
¾ lb minced beef
1 tablespoon freshly chopped parsley
Pinch of powdered mace
½ teaspoon dried thyme
2 tablespoons tomato ketchup
½ teaspoon salt
¼ teaspoon pepper
1 egg, beaten
4 tablespoons fresh breadcrumbs

Preheat the oven to 350°F, Gas Mark 4.

Cut the marrow in half and scoop out the seeds. Peel and finely chop the onion, then place it with all the remaining ingredients in a mixing bowl and blend well together.

Fill the two halves of the marrow with the stuffing and place them together again. Wrap the marrow in foil, or greased greaseproof paper, place in a baking dish and bake for about 1 hour, or until the marrow is tender. Serve with a plain white or cheese sauce (see page 44).

COTTAGE PIE

Serves 4

1 lb cold cooked meat
1 large onion
2 oz margarine
1 oz flour
½ pint beef stock
½ teaspoon Worcestershire sauce
Salt and pepper
1½ lb potatoes
Milk

Preheat the oven to 400°F, Gas Mark 6.

Mince the meat finely, peel and chop the onion. To make the sauce melt 1 oz of the margarine and fry the onion. Stir in the flour and fry for half a minute. Add the stock gradually and bring to the boil, stirring, until thickened and smooth. Add the Worcestershire sauce, salt and pepper. Mix the minced meat with the sauce and place the mixture in a pie dish.

Peel and boil the potatoes, drain them and mash with the remaining margarine and a little milk, spread over the meat, mark with a fork and bake for about 25 minutes, or until the top is golden brown.

SAVOURY BAKE

Serves 4

½ lb carrots
½ lb potatoes
6 oz to 8 oz cooked cold meat
4 oz medium oatmeal
1 egg, beaten
4 tablespoons milk
Salt and pepper
1 teaspoon mixed dried herbs
½ oz margarine
1 tomato
2 oz cheese, grated

Preheat the oven to 350°F, Gas Mark 4. Grease an 8 inch square shallow baking tin.

Peel and grate the carrots and the potatoes. Chop the cooked meat; mix into the carrot mixture with the oatmeal, egg, milk, salt and pepper and herbs.

Press into the tin, dot the top with the margarine, and bake for 1 hour. Slice the tomato, arrange over the top of the savoury bake. Sprinkle over the cheese and bake for a further 5 minutes. Cut into squares and serve with cheese sauce (see page 44).

STUFFED ONIONS WITH BEEF AND MUSHROOM FILLING

Serves 4

4 large onions
1 stick celery
¼ lb mushrooms
1 oz margarine
¾ lb minced beef
2 teaspoons freshly chopped parsley
1 teaspoon dried tarragon
1 tablespoon tomato ketchup
Salt and pepper
Parsley, to garnish

Peel the onions and parboil them in plenty of boiling water for 15 minutes. Drain off the liquid and scoop out the centres of each onion. Chop the onion which has been scooped out. Preheat the oven to 350°F, Gas Mark 4. Grease an ovenproof dish.

Wash and trim the celery and mushrooms and chop into small pieces. Melt the margarine in a frying pan and fry the mushrooms and celery lightly. Stir in the meat and fry for a few minutes. Mix in the scooped out onion, herbs, tomato ketchup, salt and pepper. Fill each onion with the mixture, piling it up well. (Any mixture which doesn't fit into the onions can be cooked in the dish around them.) Place them in the greased dish and bake for 1 hour, or until the onions are cooked and browned. If the meat starts to brown too much, cover the dish with foil. Serve with gravy or spiced Tomato Sauce (see page 44). Garnish with parsley.

CHICKEN PASTIES

Makes 8 small pasties

This recipe will make a little left over chicken go a long way.

½ lb cooked chicken
1 small onion
1 oz margarine
½ oz flour
¼ pint milk
¼ lb mushrooms
Pinch of cayenne pepper
Salt
1 (7½ oz) packet frozen flaky or puff pastry, thawed

Mince or finely chop the chicken. Peel and finely chop the onion. Melt the margarine in a saucepan and light fry the onion. Stir in the flour and cook for ½ a minute. Remove from the heat and add the milk gradually. Bring to the boil, stirring, until thickened and smooth. Wash, trim and chop the mushrooms and stir into the sauce with the chicken, cayenne pepper and salt to taste. Leave the sauce to cool. Preheat the oven to 425°F, Gas Mark 7.

Roll out the pastry on a lightly floured surface and cut out into 4 inch diameter rounds. Divide the sauce between the rounds, a little to one side of the centre. Damp the edges of the pastry and fold them over, sealing them well. Brush the pasties with a little milk and bake near the top of the preheated oven for about 20 minutes, or until golden brown.

SAUSAGE PIE

Serves 4

In this dish the pie crust is not pastry, but sausagemeat. Some grated cheese can be sprinkled in between the vegetable layers to make it a little different.

1½ lb sausagemeat
6 oz carrots
2 medium-sized potatoes
¼ lb fresh or frozen peas
1 small onion
1 tomato
1 teaspoon mixed herbs
Salt and pepper
1 oz margarine
Milk
Parsley to garnish

Grease a 9 inch shallow pie dish or tin. On a floured surface, roll out three quarters of the sausagemeat to a circle and line the pie dish with it.

Peel and slice the carrots and potatoes; cook them both in boiling salted water for 5 minutes. Drain them well. Cook the peas and drain them.

Preheat the oven to 375°F, Gas Mark 5. Peel and chop the onion finely, slice the tomato. Arrange the carrots, potatoes, onion, peas, and tomato slices in layers in the lined pie plate or tin, sprinkling over the herbs, seasoning, and small pieces of the margarine. Roll out the remaining sausagemeat and use to cover the top of the pie. Pinch the edges well together and make a hole in the top for the steam to escape. Brush over the top with milk and bake in the preheated oven for 45 minutes to 1 hour and serve hot, with a cheese sauce (see page 44). Garnish the pie with parsley.

ONE-POT STEW

Serves 4 to 5

This would be a good recipe to do in a pressure cooker. As it is a slow-cooking dish you can use cheaper cuts of meat such as neck of lamb or stewing steak.

1½ lb onions
1½ lb potatoes
2 oz margarine
3 carrots
1 lb stewing steak
3 pints beef stock
Salt and pepper
½ small cabbage
4 oz pearl barley
½ teaspoon Worcestershire sauce

Peel and slice the onions. Peel the potatoes and cut them up into chunks. Melt the margarine in a large saucepan and gently cook the onions, with the lid on, for 5 minutes. Put the potatoes in the casserole with the onions. Peel the carrots and cut into lengthwise pieces and add to the casserole. Leave all the vegetables to cook gently in the casserole, with the lid on, for 3 minutes.

Trim the meat and cut up into mouth-sized pieces. Add the meat to the casserole, fry lightly and pour in the stock. Season with salt and pepper. Cover the saucepan and bring slowly to the boil, then turn down the heat and cook very gently for about 1½ hours, stirring occasionally, until the meat is almost tender. Wash and shred the cabbage leaves and stir in for the last 30 to 45 minutes of cooking time, with the pearl barley and the Worcestershire sauce, until the stew is thickened.

SPRING GREENS AND BACON WITH EGG SAUCE

Serves 4

This is a traditional Irish dish.

1½ lb spring greens or purple sprouting broccoli
1 small onion or 2 tablespoons finely chopped chives
1½ oz margarine
1 oz flour
½ pint milk
Salt and pepper
2 hard-boiled eggs, chopped
4 to 8 rashers bacon

Wash the greens then shred in thin slices. Cook in a little boiling salted water for 10 minutes. Drain well in a colander. Peel and finely chop the onion if used.

To make the sauce melt the margarine in a saucepan and fry the onion until soft; stir in the flour and cook for half a minute. Remove from the heat and stir in the milk a little at a time.

Stir in the chives, if used. Bring to the boil, stirring, until thickened and smooth, then simmer for a further 2 minutes. Season with salt and pepper, and stir in the chopped hard-boiled eggs.

Remove the rind from the bacon and fry the bacon in a frying pan; remove from the pan and keep the bacon warm. Add the drained greens and fry very lightly, turning them continuously until piping hot, being careful not to burn the greens. Serve in a dish topped with the bacon rashers, with the sauce separately. This dish is particularly good served with potatoes boiled in their skins.

BASIC WHITE SAUCE

Makes ½ pint

1 oz margarine
1 oz flour
½ pint milk, or half milk and fish or vegetable stock
Salt and pepper

Melt the margarine in a saucepan, add the flour, and cook until it bubbles. Remove from the heat, stir in the liquid, gradually. Bring to the boil, stirring continuously, until thickened and smooth. Simmer for a further 2 minutes, remove from the heat and season to taste with salt and pepper or any of the following additions:

CHEESE SAUCE: add 3 oz grated cheese and stir over a low heat until the cheese is melted, but do not allow to boil again.

MUSTARD SAUCE: stir in 2 teaspoons made mustard.

PARSLEY SAUCE: stir in 2 heaped table-spoons freshly chopped parsley.

TOMATO SAUCE: stir in 2 tablespoons tomato ketchup.

ONION SAUCE: fry one finely chopped or sliced medium-sized onion in the margarine until soft. Add the flour, and continue as directed. After the sauce has thickened, simmer for about 10 minutes, stirring often.

SPICED TOMATO SAUCE

1 medium-sized onion
½ oz margarine
1 bay leaf
Sprig of thyme or ½ teaspoon dried thyme
4 peppercorns
1 (14 oz) tin tomatoes
2 tablespoons vinegar
1 teaspoon flour or cornflour

Peel and chop the onion. Melt the margarine and fry the onion, bay leaf, thyme and peppercorns. Fry for 5 minutes, and then add the tomatoes and vinegar and 4 fluid oz of water. Simmer gently for 15 minutes. Rub the mixture through a sieve. Return to the sauce-pan and reheat.

Mix the flour or cornflour with a little of the sauce; stir into the remaining sauce and bring to the boil, stirring continuously, until thickened. Simmer for a further 2 minutes.

Fish

The recipes in this section use the less expensive fresh fish like herrings, mackerel and cod, or tinned ones like sardine and salmon. Fish is not only nourishing, but a little can be made to go a long way if it is mixed with other ingredients to make fish cakes, served in a white sauce and topped with mashed potato, or encased in pastry like a fish envelope.

MACKEREL AND CHUTNEY PIE

Serves 4

Two (7 oz) tins mackerel
Salt and pepper
2 oz margarine
1 oz flour
Milk
2 eggs, beaten
2 tablespoons chutney
1 lb potatoes
2 oz cheese, grated
Tomato slices, to garnish

Strain the juice from the tins of mackerel. Flake the mackerel, place in the bottom of a greased pie dish and sprinkle with salt and pepper. Preheat the oven to 350°F, Gas Mark 4. Melt 1 oz of the margarine in a saucepan, stir in the flour and cook for half a minute. Remove from the heat and add ½ pint of milk gradually. Return to the heat and bring to the boil, stirring continuously, until thickened and smooth. Simmer for 3 minutes, remove from the heat and beat in the eggs and chutney. Season to taste and pour over the mackerel. Bake in the preheated oven for 40 minutes, or until set.

Peel and boil the potatoes; drain them well and mash with the remaining 1 oz of margarine, a little milk and salt and pepper. Spread evenly over the mackerel with a fork and sprinkle the cheese over the top. Grill until the top is golden brown. Garnish with tomato slices.

FISH PIE

For four

1½ lb potatoes
2 to 3 oz cheese
2 oz margerine
½ pint plus 2 tablespoons milk
¾ lb white fish
1½ oz flour
2 tablespoons freshly chopped parsley
Salt and pepper

Grease a 1½ to 2 pint pie dish.
Peel and boil the potatoes; drain them well and mash.
Grate the cheese and mix into the potatoe with ½ oz
of the margerine and 2 tablespoons of the milk.
Place the fish in a saucepan with the remaining ½ pint
of the milk, bring to the boil and simmer gently for
10 minutes or until the fish flakes easily when tested with
a fork. Strain off milk and reserve. Flake fish with a
fork, removing any skin and bones. Preheat oven to 400°F,
Gas Mark 6.
Melt remaining ½ oz margerine in a saucepan, add flour
and cook for ½ minute. Remove from heat. Make reserved
milk up to ¾ pint with water and stir into the flour mixture
gradually. Return to the heat and bring to boil, stirring
continuously until thickened and smooth. Mix in flaked
fish, parsley, and some salt and pepper to taste. Pour into
the pie dish.
Spread the potatoes over the fish with a fork and bake
for about 20 minutes, or until the top is golden brown.

FISH CAKES IN THE OVEN

Serves 4

¾ lb cod or other white fish
1 lb potatoes
1 small onion
1 oz margarine
2 teaspoons freshly chopped parsley
⅛ teaspoon ground mace
Salt and pepper
Milk
Browned breadcrumbs (see page 65)

Place the fish in a saucepan with sufficient water to just cover. Bring to the boil and simmer gently for 10 minutes, or until the flesh flakes easily when tested with a fork. Drain off the liquid. Flake the fish with a fork, removing any skin and bones.

Peel and boil the potatoes; drain them and mash well, and see that they are free from lumps. Peel and finely chop the onion. Mix the fish and potatoes together, add the margarine, onion, parsley, mace, salt and pepper, with a little milk to moisten if necessary, (if too stiff they will taste dry). Preheat the oven to 400°F, Gas Mark 6.

Turn the mixture on to a floured surface and form into a roll. Cut into slices and shape each into neat rounds. Dip in a little milk and roll in browned breadcrumbs to coat them.

Place on a well greased baking tray and bake for 20 to 30 minutes, or until golden brown. Serve with parsley sauce (see page 44).

SALMON AND NUTMEG FLAN

Serves 4

Potato Crust:
1 lb potatoes
½ oz margarine
1 oz flour
Salt and pepper
3 oz cheese, grated
Filling:
1 oz margarine
1½ oz flour
½ pint milk
1 (7 oz) tin salmon or tuna
1 egg
Grated nutmeg

Peel and boil the potatoes. When cooked strain them and add the margarine, flour and salt and pepper. Mash all together thoroughly. Grease a 1½ pint pie dish and press in the potato mixture to line the sides and base. Smooth the bottom of the potato crust with a knife. Sprinkle the cheese over the potato shell and press in lightly. Lightly brown under the grill. Preheat the oven to 400°F, Gas Mark 6.

To make the filling: melt 1 oz of the margarine in a saucepan, stir in the flour and cook for half a minute. Remove from the heat and add the milk gradually. Return to the heat and cook, stirring, until thickened and smooth. Drain and flake the salmon or tuna.

Beat the egg and stir into the sauce with the salmon or tuna, add salt and pepper to taste. Pour into the potato crust and sprinkle with nutmeg. Bake for 20 to 25 minutes, or until firm and golden.

FISH ENVELOPE

Serves 4

Any kind of fish can be used for this recipe.

¾ lb white fish
½ oz margarine
½ oz flour
1 level teaspoon paprika
Salt
1 tablespoon freshly chopped parsley
1 (7½ oz) packet frozen flaky or puff pastry, thawed or 8 oz shortcrust pastry (see page 65)
Milk
Parsley, to garnish

Place the fish in a saucepan with sufficient water to just cover. Bring to the boil and simmer gently for 10 minutes, or until the flesh flakes easily when tested with a fork. Drain off the liquid, reserving ¼ of a pint, and flake the fish, removing any skin and bones. Preheat the oven to 400°F, Gas Mark 6.

Melt the margarine in a saucepan, stir in the flour and cook for half a minute. Remove from the heat and stir in the fish liquid gradually.

Return to the heat and bring to the boil, stirring continuously, until thickened and smooth. Mix in the flaked fish, paprika, salt and parsley. Allow to cool.

Roll out the pastry on a lightly floured surface and trim to a 10 inch square. Put it on a dampened baking tray, and place the cooled filling in the centre of the pastry square. Moisten the edges with water and fold the corners of the square into the centre to make an envelope. Press the edges well together and leave a small hole in the middle for the steam to escape.

Decorate the top of the pie with pastry 'leaves' made from the pastry trimmings. Brush the pastry with milk and bake for about 30 minutes or until the pastry is golden brown. Serve hot with parsley sauce (see page 44).

CREAMED FISH AND LEEKS

Serves 6

A slightly more extravagant dish, but a tasty one for special occasions.

1½ lb fillet of white fish
1 tablespoon vinegar
1 lb leeks
1½ oz margarine
1½ oz flour
½ pint milk
2 eggs, hard boiled
3 oz cheese, grated
Salt and pepper

Skin the fish and place in a saucepan with sufficient water to just cover. Add the vinegar, then bring to the boil and simmer gently for 10

49

"*What are you doing, Mummy?*"
"*Digging for victory.*"
"*How deep down is that?*"

DRAWN BY BEAUCHAMP.

minutes, or until the flesh flakes easily when tested with a fork.

Wash the leeks, trim, slice and cook them in a little salted water until they are just tender.

Drain the fish and leeks, reserving the liquids. Flake the fish, removing any bones. Preheat the oven to 375°F, Gas Mark 5.

Make the fish and leek liquid up to $\frac{1}{2}$ pint, adding water if necessary. Melt the margarine in a saucepan, stir in the flour and cook for $\frac{1}{2}$ a minute. Remove from the heat and stir in the cooking liquid and the milk, gradually. Return to the heat and bring to the boil, stirring continuously, until thickened and smooth. Mix in the flaked fish and pieces of leek. Pour the mixture into a pie dish.

Chop the eggs and sprinkle over the fish and sauce mixture. Sprinkle the grated cheese on top and place in the preheated oven. Bake for about 15 minutes, or until all the ingredients are well heated through.

HERRING PIE

Serves 4

'Of all the fish that swim the sea' runs the old saying, 'the herring is the king.'

1 medium-sized onion
$\frac{1}{2}$ lb raw potato, grated
$\frac{1}{2}$ lb raw apple, grated
$\frac{1}{4}$ teaspoon nutmeg
Salt and pepper
1 teaspoon lemon juice
4 herrings
1 (7$\frac{1}{2}$ oz) packet flaky or puff pastry, thawed or 6 oz shortcrust pastry (see page 65)
Milk

Preheat the oven to 400°F, Gas Mark 6. Grease a 9-inch pie dish.

Peel and chop the onion and arrange half the potato, apple and onion in the pie dish. Sprinkle on the nutmeg, seasoning and lemon juice.

Bone the herrings, wash and dry with kitchen paper. Lay the herrings on top of the potato mixture.

Role out the pastry on a lightly floured surface, making it a little bit larger than the top of the dish.

Put a thin strip of pastry on to the dampened rim of the pie dish, moisten it and cover the top with the pastry lid, making a small hole in the top for the steam to escape. Trim off the surplus pastry, seal the edges. Decorate the top of the pie with pastry 'leaves' made from the pastry trimmings. Brush the pastry with milk and bake in the preheated oven for about 30 minutes or until the pastry is golden brown.

SARDINES WITH CHEESE

Serves 2

A quickly made, and tasty supper dish.

1 (3¼ oz) tin sardines
2 to 3 oz grated cheese
Cayenne pepper
Browned breadcrumbs (see page 65)

Preheat the oven to 425°F, Gas Mark 7. Grease a shallow ovenproof dish.

Remove the sardine tails and the large bones. Place in a greased ovenproof dish. Sprinkle over the grated cheese and season with cayenne pepper. Sprinkle with enough browned breadcrumbs to lightly cover. Place in the preheated oven and bake for about 15 minutes. Serve hot.

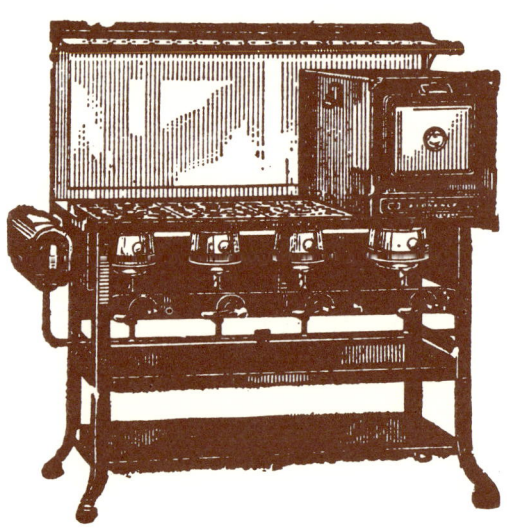

Cauliflower and Tomato Pie, page 58

Vegetable Stew with
Cheese Dumplings, page 59

Baker's Tart, page 61

Vegetable Loaf, page 58

Potato and Onion Pie, page 59

Egg and Potato Casserole,
page 60

Carrot Croquettes,
page 62

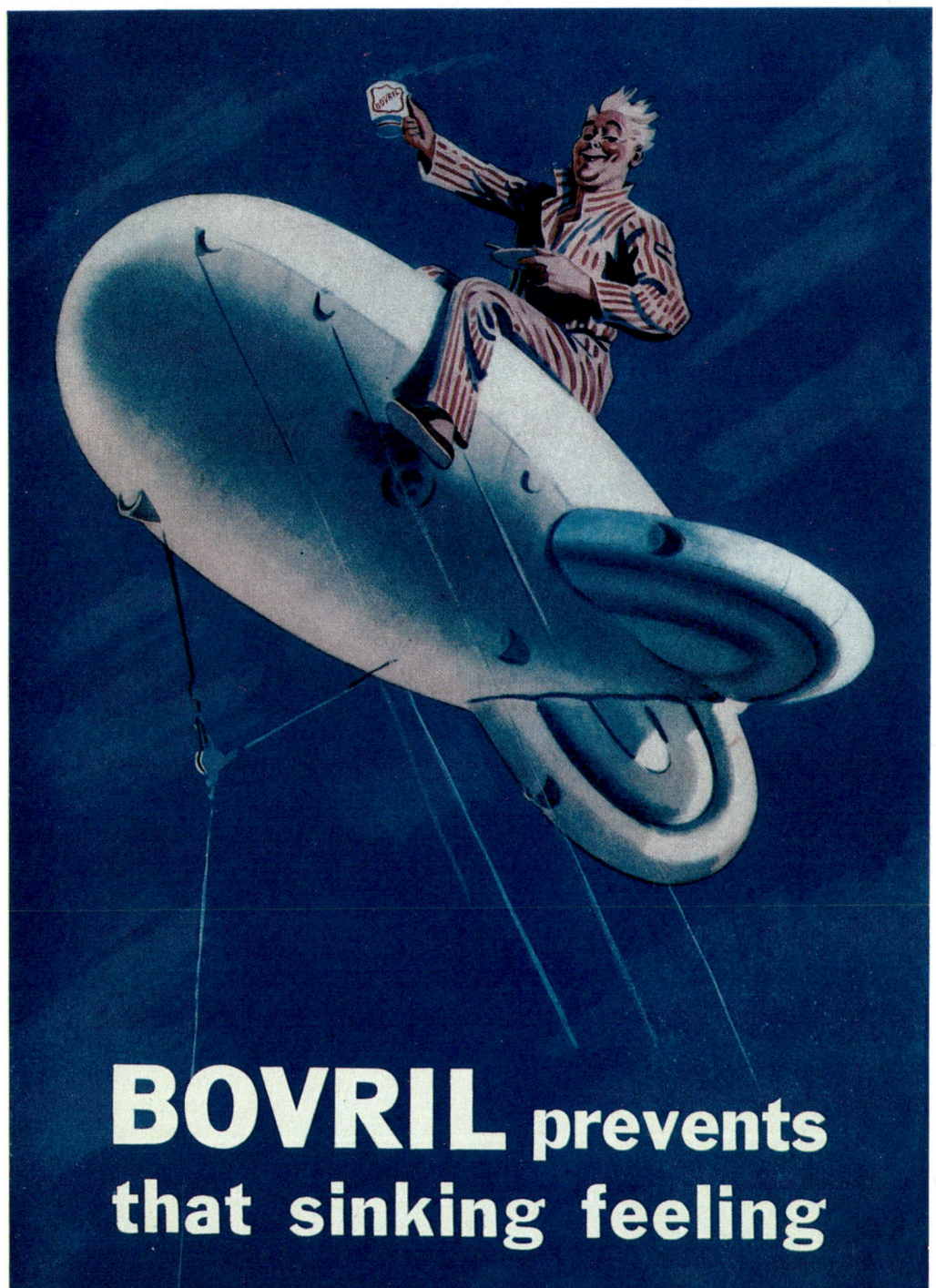

BOVRIL prevents that sinking feeling

Egg and Cheese

Eggs or cheese mixed with vegetables are the basis for many interesting, tasty and economical main meals and supper dishes. In the next few pages the recipes include a vegetable stew served with cheese dumplings, an egg and potato casserole and Baker's Tart which is quick to prepare, attractive to look at and a little different.

IRISH POTATO CAKES OR FADGE

Makes 8

1 lb potatoes
½ teaspoon salt
2 oz plain flour
Margarine, for frying

Peel and boil the potatoes, then drain them well and mash. Mix together the potato, salt and enough of the flour to make a stiff dough. Pat or roll out on a floured surface to a circle about ¼ inch thick and cut into 8 triangles.

Melt a little margarine on a hot griddle or in a heavy-based saucepan, and fry the potato cakes, turning once until brown on both sides. Serve hot.

VEGETABLE LOAF

Serves 4

This is a good and delicious way of using up leftover vegetables.

1 lb cooked mixed root vegetables
½ lb cooked mashed potatoes
1 oz butter
4 oz cheese
1 oz fresh breadcrumbs
Salt and pepper
1 teaspoon made mustard

Preheat the oven to 400°F, Gas Mark 6. Grease a 1 lb loaf tin and line the bottom with greaseproof paper.

Chop the vegetables finely and mix them with the mashed potato and butter. Grate the cheese and stir 3 oz of the cheese into the vegetables with the breadcrumbs, salt and

pepper and mustard. Place in the loaf tin. Cover with greased greaseproof paper and bake for 45 minutes. Leave to become cold in the tin to make it easier for turning out. Turn the loaf out on to a baking tray, sprinkle over the remaining 1 oz of cheese and return to the oven to warm through and brown the cheese. Serve with a green vegetable and cheese sauce (see page 44).

CAULIFLOWER AND TOMATO PIE

Serves 4

1 medium-sized cauliflower
1 medium-sized onion
1 oz margarine
½ lb tomatoes
4 oz cheese
Salt and pepper
1 (7½ oz) packet flaky or puff pastry, thawed
Milk for glazing

Preheat the oven to 425°F, Gas Mark 7. Grease a 2 pint pie dish.

Trim the cauliflower and break into florets. Cook in boiling salted water until just tender. (Do not overcook the cauliflower.) Peel and chop the onion. Melt the margarine and fry the onion lightly. Slice the tomatoes and grate the cheese.

Place a pie funnel in the centre of the dish and fill with alternate layers of cauliflower, onion, sliced tomatoes and cheese. Season with salt and pepper.

Roll out the pastry a little bit larger than the top of the dish on a lightly floured surface. Put a thin strip of pastry around the dampened rim of the pie dish, moisten it, and cover the top with the pastry lid. Trim off surplus pastry, seal the edges, brush with milk and decorate the top with pastry 'leaves' made from the pastry trimmings. Bake for 25 to 30 minutes, or until the pastry is golden brown.

VEGETABLE STEW WITH CHEESE DUMPLINGS

Serves 4

Saving fuel is a sure way to save money too. Here is a one-pot nourishing dish.

2 medium-sized onions
2 tomatoes
3 sticks celery
2 large carrots
1 small turnip or swede
2 large potatoes
2 oz margarine
Chicken stock
1 teaspoon salt
½ level teaspoon pepper
Dumplings:
4 oz self-raising flour
¼ teaspoon salt
1½ oz shredded suet
1 tablespoon freshly chopped parsley
2 oz cheese, grated
½ teaspoon dried sage

Peel and slice the onions; cut the tomatoes into quarters; wash and slice the celery. Peel the carrots and turnip or swede and potatoes and cut into small dice. Melt the margarine in a large saucepan and lightly fry the vegetables, except the tomatoes.

Pour in just enough stock to cover; add the salt and pepper. Cover and cook for 15 minutes.

To make the dumplings mix together all the ingredients with sufficient water to make a soft, not sticky dough. Form the dough into small dumplings.

Add the tomatoes to the stew. Drop the dumplings in the stew; cover and cook for a further 20 minutes.

POTATO AND ONION PIE

Serves 3 to 4

When tomatoes are in season, peel or slice one or two and add to the layers of potato and onion for an extra delicious flavour. This makes an excellent supper dish.

1 lb onions
1 lb potatoes
2 teaspoons freshly chopped sage or ½ teaspoon dried sage
Salt and pepper
1 oz margarine
½ pint milk
1 egg

Preheat the oven to 325°F, Gas Mark 3.

Peel and slice the onions and parboil for 10 minutes in boiling salted water. Peel and slice the potatoes and parboil in salted water for 10 minutes. Drain both the onion and the potato.

Grease a pie dish and arrange the sliced onion and potato in layers with a sprinkling of sage and seasoning and tiny pieces of the margarine between each. Finish with a layer of potatoes. Beat together the milk and the egg and pour carefully into the dish with the layered vegetables. Bake for 45 minutes, or until the mixture is set and the potatoes browned.

Egg and Potato Casserole

Serves 4

1½ lbs potatoes
Butter
2 tablespoons milk
3 oz cheese, grated
Salt and pepper
4 eggs
Freshly chopped parsley

Peel and boil the potatoes, drain them well and mash. Beat in 1 oz butter, the milk, cheese and salt and pepper. Preheat the oven to 350°F, Gas Mark 4. Grease an ovenproof dish.

Place the potato mixture in the ovenproof dish. Using the back of a large spoon, make four evenly spaced hollows in the potato, for the eggs. Break each egg seperately into a cup and carefully slip each one into the prepared hollows.

Top each egg with a small piece of butter. Bake in the oven until the potato is well heated and the eggs lightly set, then sprinkle the eggs with chopped parsley, and serve.

CHEESE AND POTATO PUFFS

Serves 4

To make a balanced and colourful meal, serve
these with vegetables such as carrots, peas,
beans or red cabbage.

1¼ lb potatoes
1 egg
1 oz margarine
3 to 4 oz cheese, grated
Salt and pepper
Grated nutmeg

Peel and boil the potatoes until they are
tender but not mushy. Preheat the oven to
425°F, Gas Mark 7. Grease a baking tray.
Drain the cooked potatoes well, put back the
lid and allow to steam for a few moments over a
very low heat. Separate the yolk from the
white of the egg.

Mash the potatoes, then, with a wooden
spoon, beat in the margarine, egg yolk and

grated cheese. Season with salt and pepper and
grated nutmeg.

Beat the egg white in a basin until it is stiff
and then lightly stir into the potato mixture.
Place in rough heaps on the greased baking
tray. Bake in the oven for 15 to 20 minutes.

BAKER'S TART

Serves 4

Use the part of the cottage loaf you scoop out
to make useful browned breadcrumbs (see
page 65), or make into fresh breadcrumbs.

1 large onion
1 large potato
3 tomatoes
4 to 6 oz cheese
1 medium-sized cottage loaf
1 egg
2 teaspoons milk
Salt and pepper

Preheat the oven to 400°F, Gas Mark 6.
Peel and slice the onion and potato and cook
in a little water until tender; drain well. Slice
the tomatoes. Grate the cheese. Cut the top off
the cottage loaf and scoop out the soft crumbs
from the inside of the loaf, so leaving a basket
of crust. Beat the egg and milk and brush all
over the inside of the bread 'basket'. Place on
the baking tray.

Fill the inside with layers of sliced onion,
potato, tomato and cheese, sprinkling with
salt and pepper and finishing off with a thick
layer of cheese. Place in the preheated oven
and bake for about 25 minutes, until warmed
through. Serve in wedges.

CHEESE AND ONION PASTIES

Makes 2 pasties

2 oz cheese
1 medium-sized onion
Salt and pepper
4 oz shortcrust pastry (see page 65)

Preheat the oven to 400°F, Gas Mark 6.

Grate the cheese. Peel and chop the onion and mix together with the cheese and salt and pepper.

Divide the pastry in half and roll each half into a circle on a lightly floured surface. Divide the cheese mixture in half and put one half in the centre of each pastry circle. Moisten the edge of each circle with water, bring the edges together, pressing them to seal. Place on a baking tray and bake in the preheated oven for about 25 minutes, or until golden brown. Serve hot or cold.

CARROT CROQUETTES

Makes about 20

1 lb carrots
½ lb potatoes
4 oz cheese
½ teaspoon salt
Pepper
2 teaspoons made mustard
5 oz medium oatmeal
Oatmeal, for coating
Margarine for frying
Parsley to garnish

Peel and finely grate the carrots and potatoes. Grate the cheese and mix in with the vegetables. Stir in the salt and pepper, mus-tard and oatmeal, to form a fairly stiff mixture.

Form into croquettes, coat each in a little oatmeal, and fry in a little margarine, turning once, until crisp and golden. Drain well. Garnish with parsley.

SWEETCORN AND POTATO PIE

Serves 4

A tasty lunch or supper dish. Serve with cheese sauce.

1 lb potatoes
1 large onion
1 medium-sized tin sweetcorn
2 level tablespoons flour
½ teaspoon salt
¼ teaspoon pepper
3 fluid oz milk
2 tablespoons browned breadcrumbs (see page 65)
½ oz margarine

Preheat the oven to 350°F, Gas Mark 4.

Peel the potatoes and cut them into thin slices. Grease a pie dish and half fill with the sliced potatoes, reserving some for the top layer. Peel and slice the onion and place over the potatoes. Drain the sweetcorn and put in the dish on top of the potatoes. Put another layer of potatoes on top.

Mix together the flour, salt and pepper, and sprinkle over the potatoes. Pour over the milk and then top with the browned breadcrumbs. Cut the margarine into small pieces and dot over the top.

Bake in the preheated oven for about 2 hours. Serve hot with cheese sauce (see page 44).

BRUSSELS SPROUTS WITH CHEESE

Serves 4

1 lb Brussels sprouts
Butter
Salt and pepper
Grated nutmeg
$\frac{3}{4}$ pint milk
1 small onion or shallot
2 cloves
Piece of mace
Sprig of thyme or $\frac{1}{4}$ teaspoon dried thyme
3 oz cheese
$1\frac{1}{2}$ oz margarine
$1\frac{1}{2}$ oz flour

Trim the outer leaves from the sprouts and cook the sprouts in a little boiling salted water, until just tender (do not overcook). Drain well, toss in a little butter and season with salt and pepper and nutmeg. Spread the sprouts out in a shallow ovenproof dish.

To make the sauce place $\frac{3}{4}$ pint of milk in a saucepan with a small onion or shallot stuck with the cloves, a little grated nutmeg or a piece of mace, salt, pepper and the thyme. Bring it to the boil, remove from the heat and let it infuse for 20 minutes and then strain. Grate the cheese.

Melt the margarine in another saucepan, stir in the flour and cook for half a minute. Remove from the heat and stir in the strained milk gradually. Return to the heat and bring to the boil, stirring continuously, until thickened and smooth. Simmer for 2 minutes; stir in half of the cheese and pour over the sprouts. Sprinkle the remaining cheese over the top and warm through and brown under the grill.

SHORTCRUST PASTRY

Quantity	4 oz	6 oz	8 oz
Plain flour	4 oz	6 oz	8 oz
Salt	Pinch	Pinch	Pinch
Margarine	1 oz	1½ oz	2 oz
Cooking fat	1 oz	1½ oz	2 oz
Cold water	4 teaspoons	6 teaspoons	8 teaspoons

Place the flour and salt in a mixing bowl. Rub in the margarine and cooking fat until the mixture resembles fine breadcrumbs. Mix in the water and press lightly together to make a firm dough. Use as required.

SUETCRUST PASTRY

Quantity	4 oz	6 oz	8 oz
Self-raising flour	4 oz	6 oz	8 oz
Salt	¼ level teaspoon	½ level teaspoon	½ level teaspoon
Shredded suet	2 oz	3 oz	4 oz
Cold water	Approx 3 to 4 tablespoons	Approx 5 to 6 tablespoons	Approx 7 to 8 tablespoons

Mix together the flour, salt and suet in a mixing bowl. Add sufficient water to make a soft, but not sticky dough. Use as required.

TO MAKE BROWNED BREADCRUMBS

Don't throw away stale pieces of bread or crusts. They are useful for several of the recipes in the book.

When you have finished with the oven, and while it is still warm, pop the bread on to a baking tray and leave in the oven until it is crisp. Then put it into a polythene bag and crush into breadcrumbs with a rolling pin. Store the breadcrumbs in an airtight tin or jar.

THE PUDDINGS OF THE PAST

Whatever has happened to the good old British pudding? Where now are the puddings that childhood memories are made of – the Spotted Dick, the treacle pud, the fruit crumbles and the trifles? Perhaps because in recent times we've had more money to spend on substantial main courses a filling pudding has been unnecessary. But now times are tighter and main meals less elaborate, so perhaps the time is ripe for the substantial, comforting pudding to make a come-back. Let's start the revival.

Steamed and Baked

The recipes that follow should be passed over quickly by anyone trying to whittle down their waistline! In this section you will find all the old favourite puddings like treacle layer, steamed chocolate and bread and butter, plus some less familiar but equally delicious ones like coffee toffee, honey walnut and Jack Horner pudding.

BREAD AND BUTTER PUDDING

Serves 4

Slices of thin bread and butter (about 4 oz)
4 oz raisins
2 oz sugar
2 eggs
1 pint milk
Grated nutmeg

Butter a 2 pint pie dish. Cut the slices of bread into triangles. Layer the bread in the dish, sprinkling the raisins and sugar between each layer. Beat up the eggs, mix with the milk, pour over the pudding and allow to stand for 10 minutes. Preheat the oven to 350°F, Gas Mark 4.

Sprinkle the pudding with a little grated nutmeg and bake for 35 to 40 minutes, or until golden brown.

SPICED BREAD PUDDING

Serves 4 to 5

The secret of making a good bread pudding of this type lies in soaking the bread just long enough to get moist but not soggy. If soaked for too long the pudding will be wet and stodgy inside.

4 thick rounds of stale bread
1½ oz self-raising flour
Pinch of salt
1 heaped teaspoon mixed spice
3 oz chopped prunes, dates, sultanas or currants
1½ oz sugar
2 eggs
2 oz margarine
¼ level teaspoon bicarbonate of soda
2 tablespoons milk

Preheat the oven to 400°F, Gas Mark 6. Grease a 7 inch square by 1 inch deep cake tin.

Break the bread into pieces and soak in cold water for 5 minutes. Squeeze dry, place into a mixing bowl and break up as small as possible with a fork. Stir in the flour, salt, spice, fruit and sugar. Beat the eggs; melt the margarine, dissolve the bicarbonate of soda in the milk. Stir the eggs, margarine and milk into the bread mixture until it is smooth. Pour into the cake tin and bake for 50 to 55 minutes. Serve hot with a jam sauce (see page 88) or cold, cut into squares.

HONEY WALNUT PUDDING

Serves 4

2 oz margarine
6 fluid oz milk
4 level tablespoons honey
1 egg, beaten
2 oz walnuts
4 oz self-raising flour
2 oz browned breadcrumbs (see page 65)
2 teaspoons vanilla flavouring

Grease a 1½ pint pie dish. Preheat the oven to 350°F, Gas Mark 4. Place the margarine, milk, honey and beaten egg into a saucepan, and warm through very gently. Remove from the heat.

Chop the walnuts and mix with the flour and breadcrumbs in a mixing bowl. Add the vanilla flavouring to the milk mixture and stir into the flour mixture. Pour into the pie dish and bake for about 1 hour. Serve with warmed honey or with a lemon sauce (see page 88).

QUEEN OF PUDDINGS

Serves 4

½ pint milk
1 oz margarine
2 oz fresh white breadcrumbs
3 oz castor sugar
2 eggs
¼ teaspoon vanilla flavouring
Grated rind of 1 small lemon
2 tablespoons jam

Preheat the oven to 375°F, Gas Mark 5. Grease a 1½ pint pie dish.

Heat the milk with the margarine, stir in the breadcrumbs and 1 oz of the sugar. Leave to stand for 5 minutes. Separate the eggs, beat the yolks into the milk mixture with the vanilla flavouring and lemon rind. Pour into the prepared dish and bake for about 30 minutes or until set.

Spread the jam over the top of the pudding. Whisk the egg whites until stiff, whisk in 1 oz of the sugar, then fold in the remaining 1 oz of the sugar. Pile on top of the pudding and bake for a further 10 minutes or until golden.

RHUBARB AND ORANGE PUDDING

Serves 4

You will find that the orange rind and juice take away the acidity of the rhubarb. If you have no brown sugar, granulated can be used instead.

8 oz suetcrust pastry (see page 65)
1½ lb rhubarb
3 oz soft brown sugar
Grated rind and juice of 1 orange

Grease a 1½ pint pudding basin.

Roll out three-quarters of the suetcrust pastry into a circle large enough to line the basin.

Trim the rhubarb and cut into 1 inch lengths. Put the rhubarb into the lined pudding basin, sprinkling in the sugar and grated orange rind as you go. When the basin is full, pour over the orange juice. Roll out the remaining pastry to a circle for the lid. Dampen the edges of the pasry and press on the lid, sealing the two edges firmly together.

Cover with greased greaseproof paper, or foil, and steam over boiling water for about 1½ to 2 hours.

BRISTOL PUDDING

Serves 4

The day before you make this pudding, the prunes need to be soaked in enough water to cover them, and left overnight.

10 prunes
3 oz margarine
3 oz castor sugar
2 eggs
4 oz self-raising flour
Grated rind of half a lemon
Milk

Grease a 1½ pint pudding basin.

Drain the soaked prunes, stone and chop them. Cream the margarine and sugar together in a mixing bowl until they are light and fluffy. Beat the eggs and beat into the creamed mixture gradually, adding a little of the flour if the mixture curdles. Fold in the remaining flour, half at a time. Stir in the chopped prunes, lemon rind and a little milk, if needed, to make a soft dropping consistency.

Place the mixture in the pudding basin, cover with greased greaseproof paper or foil, and steam over boiling water for about 1½ hours. Turn out and serve with lemon and syrup sauce (see page 88).

TREACLE LAYER PUDDING

Serves 4 to 6

5 level tablespoons golden syrup
1 oz fresh breadcrumbs
Grated rind of a small lemon
1 tablespoon lemon juice
½ level teaspoon ginger
8 oz self-raising flour
Pinch of salt
4 oz shredded suet
7 to 8 tablespoons milk or water
2 cooking apples

Grease a 1½ pint pudding basin. Mix together the syrup, breadcrumbs, lemon rind and juice and ginger in a basin.

Place the flour and salt in another mixing bowl. Add the suet and mix in enough of the milk or water to give a soft, but not sticky dough. Roll out a little more than half of the dough into a circle on a lightly floured surface and line the basin with it. Spread the bottom with a little of the syrup mixture.

Peel, core and slice the apples. Place one third of the apple over the syrup mixture. Divide the remaining pastry into three pieces and roll out three circles to fit into the basin. Place one on top of the apples. Fill up with alternate layers of the syrup mixture, apple and pastry, finishing with pastry. Damp the edge of this top layer with water and press the edges firmly to seal. Cover with greased greaseproof paper or foil and steam over boiling water for 1½ to 2 hours.

71

SPOTTED DICK

Serves 4

4 oz self-raising flour
4 oz fresh white breadcrumbs
Pinch of salt
4 oz shredded suet
2 oz sugar
3 oz currants
Just over ¼ pint milk

Grease a 1½ pint pudding basin.

Sift the flour into a mixing bowl and add the breadcrumbs, salt, suet, sugar and currants. Stir in enough of the milk so the mixture drops easily from the spoon.

Place the mixture into the pudding basin. Cover the basin securely with greased grease-proof paper or foil and steam over boiling water for 1½ to 2 hours. Turn out and serve with syrup or custard.

THREE-AND-THREE PUDDING

Serves 4 to 6

1 (7½ oz) packet frozen flaky or rough puff pastry, thawed
3 large cooking apples
3 oz brown sugar or 4 tablespoons golden syrup
3 oz butter or margarine
Grated rind and juice of 1 lemon
3 eggs
3 oz castor sugar

Preheat the oven to 425°F, Gas Mark 7.

Roll out the pastry and line a 9 inch shallow pie dish; trim off the surplus pastry and decorate the edges with cut pastry leaves made from the pastry trimmings.

Peel, core and slice the apples; place in a saucepan with 3 tablespoons of water, and simmer gently until soft. Mash with a fork or rub through a sieve. Add the sugar or golden syrup, butter or margarine, lemon rind and juice.

Separate the eggs and beat the yolks into the apple mixture. Heat through until the butter has melted, but do not allow to boil. Pour into the pastry case and bake for 10 minutes, then reduce the oven temperature to 375°F, Gas Mark 5 and bake for a further 20 minutes.

Whisk the egg whites until stiff; whisk in half the castor sugar, then fold in the other half. Pile the meringue mixture on top of the pudding. Reduce the oven temperature to 350°F, Gas Mark 4 and bake the pudding for a further 15 to 20 minutes, or until the meringue is pale golden in colour.

BACHELOR'S PUDDING

Serves 4 to 6

You can make this pudding a little less rich by leaving out the butter or margarine.

Brown sugar for sprinkling
4 oz self-raising flour
2 oz butter or margarine
4 oz shredded suet
4 oz raisins
4 oz demerara sugar
4 oz fresh breadcrumbs
1 level teaspoon ground ginger
2 eggs
Milk

Grease a 1½ pint pudding basin and sprinkle the inside with a little brown sugar.

Place the flour in a mixing bowl and rub in

72

the butter or margarine until the mixture resembles fine breadcrumbs. Mix in the suet, raisins, demerara sugar, breadcrumbs and ginger. Beat the eggs and mix into the mixture with enough milk to give a soft dropping consistency.

Place the mixture in the pudding basin, cover with greased greaseproof paper or foil and steam for 1½ to 2 hours.

EVESHAM PUDDING

Serves 4

You can use either a medium-sized tin of plums for this pudding or a pound of fresh fruit such as plums, greengages, damsons or currants. It is also a good way of using up stale sponge cake. If you haven't any, use trifle sponges instead.

1 medium-sized tin of plums or 1 lb fresh fruit
4 oz cake crumbs
5 oz sugar
1 oz cornflour
½ pint milk
2 eggs
Sugar for sprinkling

If using a tin of fruit, strain off ¼ pint of the syrup and heat in a saucepan until nearly boiling. Place the cake crumbs in a basin and pour over the hot syrup. If using fresh fruit, prepare the fruit and simmer in a saucepan with 2 oz of the sugar and 6 tablespoons of water, until tender. Strain off this juice for pouring over the cake crumbs. Place the tinned or stewed fruit in the bottom of an ovenproof pie dish. Preheat the oven to 325°F, Gas Mark 3.

Blend the cornflour with 1 oz of the sugar and a little of the milk, to make a smooth paste, in a saucepan. Stir in the remaining milk gradually. Bring to the boil, stirring, until thickened and smooth, cook for a further 2 minutes.

Separate the eggs and beat the yolks into the cornflour mixture. Then mix in the soaked cake crumbs. Pour this mixture over the fruit in the pie dish.

Whisk the egg whites until stiff, whisk in 1 oz of the sugar, then fold in the remaining 1 oz. Pile the meringue mixture on top of the pudding, sprinkle over a little sugar and bake in the preheated oven for about 15 minutes, or until the meringue is pale brown.

PLUM BATTER

Serves 4

If plums are not available use cooking apples instead for this pudding.

1 lb ripe plums
4 oz plain flour
½ level teaspoon salt
1 oz sugar
1 egg
½ pint milk and water
1 oz butter
Topping:
1 oz flaked almonds
2 oz castor sugar
½ teaspoon cinnamon

Preheat the oven to 400°F, Gas Mark 6. Grease an 8 by 10 by 2 inch baking tin or dish very well.

Stone and peel the plums and cut them into pieces. Make the batter: place the flour and salt in a mixing bowl with the sugar. Make a well in the centre, then add the egg and half of the milk and water. Beat well until smooth. Then beat in the remaining milk and water gradually. Melt the butter and beat into the batter. Pour the batter into the baking tin and place the pieces of plum in it.

Mix together all the topping ingredients. Sprinkle over the plums and bake for 45 minutes to 1 hour. Serve with custard.

APRICOT SPONGE

Serves 4

The day before you make this pudding, the apricots need to be soaked in sufficient water to cover them, and left overnight.

6 oz dried apricots
6 oz castor sugar
4 oz margarine
2 eggs
5 oz self-raising flour
Milk
Sugar for sprinkling

Preheat the oven to 350°F, Gas Mark 4. Grease a 2 pint pie dish.

Drain the soaked apricots and place in the pie dish with 2 oz of the sugar and enough water to come halfway up the fruit.

Cream the margarine and the remaining 4 oz sugar together in a mixing bowl until light and fluffy. Beat the eggs and beat into the creamed mixture gradually. Sift the flour and fold in, half at a time with enough milk to give a soft dropping consistency. Spread this sponge mixture on top of the apricots. Bake in the preheated oven for about 1 hour until risen and set. Sprinkle with castor sugar and serve hot.

Among the pleasures of future peaceful days will be Turban Stoned Dates as a luscious dessert. The familiar "Turban" carton will be back in the shops as soon as conditions permit.

Brown Betty — Serves 4 to 6

2 lb cooking apples
2 oz browned breadcrumbs
3 oz brown sugar
2 oz margarine
1 lemon
Pinch of grated nutmeg
Two level teaspoons cinnamon

Preheat the oven to 350°F. Gas Mark 4. Grease an oven proof pie dish.

Peel and core the apples, then grate them coarsely. Place one third of the breadcrumbs in the bottom of the pie dish. Cover with a layer of half the grated apple. Put half the sugar over the apples and dot with half the margarine. Finely grate the rind from the lemon and squeeze the juice. Sprinkle the spices over the apple and then the lemon rind. Repeat with another layer of breadcrumbs and apples, add the remaining sugar. Top with a final layer of breadcrumbs and dot with margarine. Mix the lemon juice with 4 fluid oz of water and pour over the pudding.

Bake in the preheated oven for 45 minutes. Serve with lemon syrup sauce.

STEAMED CHOCOLATE PUDDING

Serves 4 to 6

3 oz margarine
5 level tablespoons golden syrup
1 egg
4 oz self-raising flour
1 oz cocoa powder
5 tablespoons milk
2 tablespoons blackcurrant jam

Grease a 1½ pint pudding basin.

Cream together the margarine and the syrup, beat in the egg. (The mixture may appear slightly curdled.) Sift together the flour and cocoa, fold into the creamed mixture alternately with the milk to give a soft dropping consistency. Place the jam in the bottom of the basin, and the chocolate mixture on top. Cover with greased greaseproof paper, or foil, and steam over boiling water for 1½ to 2 hours. Turn out and serve with a plain sweet sauce (see page 88).

COFFEE TOFFEE PUDDING

Serves 6 to 8

This is a very filling pudding with a crumbly texture – excellent after a fairly light main course.

3 oz margarine
4 oz sugar
1 tablespoon coffee essence, or a very strong mixture of instant coffee and water
4 oz self-raising flour
4 oz browned breadcrumbs (see page 65)
2 oz sultanas
1 egg
6 fluid oz milk

Grease a 2½ pint pudding basin.

Melt the margarine in a small saucepan, stir in the sugar and coffee essence; remove from the heat and allow to cool.

Place the flour in a mixing bowl with the browned breadcrumbs and sultanas and mix together. Beat the egg in a basin and stir in the milk and the cooled coffee mixture. Pour all of this liquid into the dry ingredients and beat with a wooden spoon until well mixed.

Place the mixture into the basin, cover with greased greaseproof paper or foil and steam over boiling water for 2 to 2½ hours. Turn out and serve with custard.

JACK HORNER PUDDING

Serves 4

An economical way of cooking a pudding, as the fruit and pastry are cooked together in a saucepan.

1 lb fresh fruit
Sugar, to sweeten
4 oz plain flour
1½ level teaspoons baking powder
¼ level teaspoon salt
1½ oz margarine
1 oz grated raw potato

Prepare the fruit and place in a medium-sized saucepan with sugar to sweeten and 4 tablespoons of water.

Mix together the flour, baking powder and salt in a mixing bowl. Rub in the margarine until the mixture resembles fine breadcrumbs. Add the potato and sufficient water (2 to 3 tablespoons) to mix to a fairly firm dough.

Roll out on a lightly floured surface to ½ inch thickness and the size in diameter of the top of the saucepan. Bring the fruit to the boil, reduce the heat, place the pastry circle on top, cover the saucepan with a lid and simmer very gently for 40 to 45 minutes. Dish up the fruit piled on the pastry.

GREAT AUNT DOROTHY'S CARROT PUDDING

Serves 4 to 6

If you are feeling extravagant, add a tablespoon or two of sherry or brandy to this pudding. The carrot should be weighed after it has been peeled and coarsely grated.

8 oz self-raising flour
4 oz shredded suet
4 oz coarsely grated carrot
4 oz currants
4 oz sultanas
1 oz sugar
1 to 2 tablespoons sherry or brandy (optional)
6 fluid oz milk

Grease a 1½ pint pudding basin.

Mix all the dry ingredients together in a mixing bowl, then stir in the sherry or brandy if used, with enough of the milk to give a fairly soft mixture. Place the mixture in the pudding basin, cover with greased greaseproof paper or foil, and steam over boiling water for 1¾ to 2 hours. Serve with custard.

PASTRY AND PIES

Really light, melt-in-the-mouth pastry combined with a delicious filling – there you have one of the classics of simple British cookery.

Cornish custard pie, Bakewell tart, apple roll slices, these are just three of the delicious pastry puddings you will find in this section.

ALMOND DATE FLAN

Serves 4 to 6

4 oz shortcrust pastry (see page 65)
Filling:
3 to 4 oz stoned dates
⅓ pint milk
1 tablespoon sugar
1 level tablespoon ground rice
2 eggs
¼ teaspoon almond flavouring

Preheat the oven to 400°F, Gas Mark 6.

Roll out the pastry on a lightly floured surface and line a 7 inch pie tin.

To make the filling: chop or slice the dates and arrange over the bottom of the pastry. Place the milk and sugar in a saucepan and bring to the boil. Sprinkle in the ground rice, stirring all the time, and simmer gently for 5 minutes, stirring frequently. Remove from the heat. Beat the eggs and stir in with the almond flavouring. Pour this mixture over the dates and bake in the preheated oven for 30 minutes.

GAINSBOROUGH TART

Serves 4

If you have a taste for coconut, you will enjoy this recipe.

6 oz shortcrust pastry (see page 65)
1 heaped tablespoon jam
1 oz butter
1 egg, beaten
2 fluid oz milk
2 oz castor sugar
4 oz desiccated coconut
¼ level teaspoon baking powder

Preheat the oven to 375°F, Gas Mark 5. Roll out the pastry on a lightly floured surface and use it to line a deep 7 inch pie plate or sandwich tin. Spread the bottom of the pastry with a little jam.

Melt the butter in a small saucepan, remove from the heat; stir in the beaten egg, milk, sugar, coconut and baking powder. Pour into the pastry case and bake for about 30 minutes or until the top is golden brown.

ANGELA'S CORNISH CUSTARD PIE

Serves 4 to 6

To bake the pastry case 'blind' line it with greaseproof paper or foil and fill with dried beans. It is best not to prick the pastry base as the filling may leak through.

6 oz shortcrust pastry (see page 65)
2 oz mixed dried fruit
2 eggs
2 tablespoons sugar
½ pint milk
Grated rind of 1 small lemon
Ground or grated nutmeg

Preheat the oven to 400°F, Gas Mark 6.

Roll out the pastry on a lightly floured surface and line an 8 inch pie tin, flan ring or sandwich tin. Bake the pastry case 'blind' for 20 minutes. Sprinkle the dried fruit over the pastry base. Beat the eggs and mix with the sugar and milk. Strain, stir in the lemon rind and pour into the pastry case. Sprinkle the top with nutmeg and bake for 10 minutes, then reduce the heat to 350°F, Gas Mark 4 for a further 25 to 35 minutes, or until the custard is set.

Butterscotch Pie

Enough for 4

6 oz shortcrust pastry
3 oz flour
1 pt milk
4 level tbsp golden syrup
1½ oz margarine
½ tsp vanilla flavouring
A little brown sugar

Preheat oven to 400°F (Gas 6). Roll out pastry on a lightly floured surface & line an 8 in flan ring or sandwich tin. Bake blind for 15 mins. Remove paper & return pastry to oven for 5 more mins. to dry out centre.

Put flour in basin & blend in a little milk to make a smooth paste. Boil rest of milk & pour into blended flour, stirring well. Return mixture to saucepan & bring to boil, stirring continuously until thickened & smooth. Cook for 4 more mins. Put syrup & marge into another saucepan & boil for a few mins without stirring until colour changes to light caramel. Stir this into sauce with the vanilla & put in pastry case.

Serve cold, sprinkled with a little brown sugar.

UNCLE IAN'S SPECIAL APPLE ROLL SLICES

Makes about 12 slices

1 lb cooking apples
2 oz brown sugar
½ teaspoon cinnamon
2 oz sultanas
8 oz shortcrust pastry (see page 65)
1 oz butter
Sugar for dredging

Peel, core and finely chop the apples. Place in a bowl and mix with the sugar, cinnamon and sultanas. Preheat the oven to 400°F, Gas Mark 6. Grease a baking tray.

Roll out the pastry on a lightly floured surface to an oblong 14 inches by 12 inches. Spread the chopped apple mixture over the pastry, dot with pieces of butter and roll up from the long sides like a roly poly. Place the roll on the baking tray and cut three quarters of the way through the roll into 1 inch thick slices.

Bake for 20 minutes, then baste with the syrup which comes from the slices. Return to the oven and bake for a further 15 minutes. Dredge with sugar and serve with custard.

CHANNEL ISLAND PLUM TART

Serves 6

For best results flaky, or puff pastry should be used, but short pastry is acceptable.

1 (7½ oz) packet frozen flaky or puff pastry, thawed
1½ lb plums
3 oz brown sugar

Roll out the pastry thinly on a lightly floured surface and line a Swiss roll tin 12 inches by 8 inches, reserving the trimmings. Halve the plums and take out the stones. Arrange the plum halves closely together, inside the pastry. Cut long, thin strips of pastry from the trimmings and use them to make a criss-cross pattern over the tart. Sprinkle the brown sugar all over and let the tart stand for 30 minutes so that the sugar may melt a little with the fruit juice. During this time, preheat the oven to 425°F, Gas Mark 7.

Bake in the preheated oven for 10 minutes then reduce the temperature to 375°F, Gas Mark 5 for a further 20 to 25 minutes until the pastry is golden and the fruit tender, but not pulpy.

Try this Delightful Summer Drink

TRY this really delightful drink for summer days—*cold* "Ovaltine." As delicious in this way as when made as a hot beverage. It not merely quenches the thirst, but refreshes and invigorates as well.

It supplies, too, the nourishment you particularly need in the summer—for ordinary hot weather foods contain little nourishment, while the need for nourishment remains much the same all the year round.

Cold "Ovaltine" is easy to prepare. Add to cold milk or milk and water. Whisk with an egg-whisk or shake in a cocktail shaker. Then you have a creamy, foaming drink—as delicious as it is refreshing. Brimful, too, of energy-giving nourishment to enable you to avoid fatigue and to keep vigorous and healthy.

'OVALTINE'
Nourishing COLD & Refreshing

Prices in Great Britain and Northern Ireland, 1/3, 2/- and 3/9 per tin.   P565

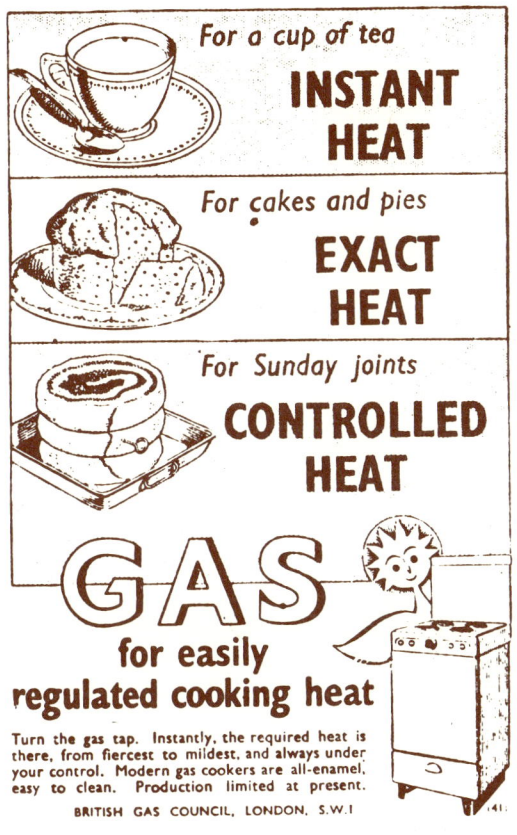

GOLDEN SQUARES

Makes 12 squares

7 level tablespoons golden syrup
2 oz fresh breadcrumbs
Rind and juice of 1 small lemon
8 oz shortcrust pastry (see page 65)
Sugar for sprinkling

Preheat the oven to 400°F, Gas Mark 6.

Mix together the golden syrup, breadcrumbs, lemon rind and juice. Divide the pastry into two equal pieces. Roll out one half on a lightly floured surface to a rectangle 8 inches by 12 inches. Place on a baking tray. Spread the golden syrup mixture to within $\frac{1}{4}$ inch of the edges.

Roll out the other piece of pastry to the same size, dampen the edges and place on top. With the back of a fork, press the edges well together to seal.

Mark the top into 12 squares with the back of a knife. Brush over with water, then sprinkle with sugar. Bake in the preheated oven for 30 minutes or until golden brown. Cut into squares when cool.

BAKEWELL TART

Serves 4 to 6

4 oz shortcrust pastry (see page 65)
Blackcurrant jam
2 oz butter
2 oz castor sugar
1 egg
¼ teaspoon almond flavouring
1 oz ground almonds or 1 oz cake crumbs to make a plainer mixture
1 oz self-raising flour
Halved blanched almonds

Preheat the oven to 375°F, Gas Mark 5.

Roll out the pastry on a lightly floured surface and line a 7 inch pie tin or sandwich tin. Spread a thin layer of jam over the base of the pastry. Cream the butter and sugar until light and creamy. Beat in the eggs gradually, then stir in the almond flavouring, ground almonds or cake crumbs and flour. Spread this mixture over the jam and scatter a few halved almonds over the top. Bake in the preheated oven for 40 minutes.

COLD DESSERTS

There is a great advantage in cold puddings that can be prepared well in advance and then left to enable you to concentrate on the main course. Some of the recipes that follow are for delicious desserts using summer fruits, others are for moulds and trifles.

Summer Pudding - Serves 6

Thick slices of white bread from a large loaf.
1½ lbs mixed soft fruits (e.g. red currants, raspberries, strawberries, blackberries).
3 oz sugar.

Grease a 1½ pint pudding basin. Remove the crusts from the slices of bread. Line the side and base of the basin with the slices, fitting them closely together so that they over-lap, trim to fit if necessary.
Cook the fruit in 2 tablespoons of water with the sugar for a few minutes only, so that the fruits do not lose their shape. Pour the fruit into the pudding basin and cover with slices of bread. Place a saucer over the top with a weight on it and leave overnight. Turn out and serve with cream, or the top of the milk, and decorate with fresh fruit.

JUNE'S CHOCOLATE TRIFLE

Serves 4

This is a delicious way of using up half a stale chocolate Swiss roll or sponge cake. If you have a leftover tinned pear, or a fresh one that needs using up, add it to the trifle – it gives an extra special flavour.

½ chocolate Swiss roll or sponge
1 packet chocolate blancmange powder
2 dessertspoons sugar
1 pint milk
1 or 2 pears
Whipping cream (for decoration)

Cut the chocolate Swiss roll or sponge into slices or cubes and place them in the bottom of a glass dish.

Make up the blancmange with the sugar and milk as directed on the packet. Allow to cool slightly.

Stir the cooled, but not set, blancmange and pour over the sponge. Leave to set.

Peel and core the fresh pears if you have one. Slice either the fresh or tinned pear.

When cold and set, decorate with the whipping cream and pear slices.

CHOCOLATE SANDWICH BLANCMANGE

Serves 6

4 oz cornflour
4 oz sugar
1 oz cocoa
2 pints milk
1½ teaspoons vanilla flavouring

Place 2 oz of the cornflour and 2 oz of the sugar in one basin, and the remaining cornflour and sugar with the cocoa in a second basin. Blend in a little of the milk with the contents of each basin to make a smooth paste. Boil the remainder of the milk and pour half into each basin, stirring well.

Pour the two mixtures into separate saucepans, bring each to the boil, stirring continuously until thickened and smooth, cook for a further 2 minutes. Allow to cool slightly, but not set. Add 1 teaspoon of vanilla to the plain blancmange, and half a teaspoon to the chocolate one. Rinse out a 2 pint jelly mould with water. Fill with alternate layers of the two mixtures. Leave to set in a cold place, then turn out.

GOOSEBERRY FOOL

Serves 4

Rhubarb can be used instead of the gooseberries; colour with a little pink food colouring instead of the green.

1 lb green gooseberries
4 oz sugar
½ oz custard powder
½ pint milk
Green food colouring
Walnut halves

Place the gooseberies, sugar and 2 tablespoons of water in a saucepan, and stew until tender. Rub through a sieve or liquidise, and cool. Blend the custard powder with 2 tablespoons of the milk in a bowl to make a smooth paste. Bring the remaining milk to the boil and

86

stir it into the blended custard powder. Return to the saucepan and bring to the boil, stirring, until thickened and smooth. Leave to cool slightly, then mix with the fruit. Stir in a few drops of green colouring to colour a pale green. Serve in individual dishes, and decorate each with a walnut half.

For an extra special treat, $\frac{1}{4}$ pint of whipped double cream can be stirred into the cooled custard as well. For a raspberry or strawberry fool the fruit should be sieved or liquidised raw and not cooked.

ORANGE MOULD

Serves 4

Jelly moulds have turned into decorative items rather than the much-used pieces of equipment they once were. For maximum effect this pudding should be made in a mould and carefully turned out before serving.

2 oz cornflour
2 oz sugar
1 pint milk
Rind and juice of $\frac{1}{2}$ an orange
$\frac{1}{2}$ oz margarine
Orange segments to decorate

Place the cornflour and sugar in a basin and blend a little of the milk to make a smooth paste. Boil the remainder of the milk and pour into the blended cornflour, stirring well. Add the orange rind and juice, return the milk mixture to the saucepan, add the margarine, and bring to the boil, stirring continuously until thickened and smooth. Cook for a further 2 minutes.

Rinse out a 1 pint jelly mould with water and pour in the orange mixture, or cool slightly and pour into a glass serving dish. Leave to set in a cold place, then turn out. Decorate with orange segments.

Giving Mother the night off

. . . by cooking the dinner for her

I have bought a sixpenny packet of Brown & Polson's Flavoured Cornflour. I'll make a Vanilla blancmange with a Strawberry sauce. That leaves Raspberry and Lemon for another time. They will nourish the boys, save Dad's money, and give Mother a new idea. One minute and the pudding's done, and it's one they'll want again!

Brown & Polson's Corn Flour *flavoured!*

BASIC SWEET SAUCE

Makes ½ pint

This recipe makes ½ pint of sweet sauce; for a pint, simply double the recipe, or halve it for ¼ of a pint.

1 level tablespoon cornflour or arrowroot
1 rounded tablespoon sugar
½ pint water (for a clear sauce) or milk

Mix together the cornflour or arrowroot with the sugar in a basin. Blend with a little of the liquid to make a smooth paste, then gradually stir in the remainder. Bring to the boil, stirring continuously, until thickened and smooth. Simmer for a further 2 minutes, stirring. Remove from the heat and add any of the following flavourings:

JAM SAUCE: make as for basic sweet sauce, but omit the sugar. When the sauce is cooked, remove from the heat and stir in 3 tablespoons jam until well blended.

LEMON SYRUP SAUCE: use 1 level tablespoon custard powder instead of cornflour, omit the sugar and make as for sweet sauce. When the sauce is cooked remove from the heat and stir in 2 tablespoons golden syrup and the grated rind and juice of half a lemon. (Orange rind and juice can be substituted for the lemon.

MARMALADE SAUCE: make as for sweet sauce, and when it is cooked, stir in 3 tablespoons marmalade.

CHOCOLATE SAUCE

Makes ½ pint

1 heaped teaspoon cocoa powder
1 oz sugar
½ pint milk or milk and water
1 oz margarine
½ oz flour
¼ level teaspoon cinnamon (optional)

Mix together the cocoa and sugar in a basin. Blend with a little of the liquid, to make a smooth paste, then gradually stir in the remainder. Melt the margarine in a saucepan, add the flour, and cook until it bubbles. Remove from the heat, stir in the blended cocoa gradually. Bring to the boil, stirring continuously, until thickened and smooth. Simmer for a further 2 minutes, stirring. Add the cinnamon if used. Serve hot.

Chocolate Sandwich Blancmange,
page 86

Summer Pudding, page 85

Gooseberry Fool,
page 86

Orange Mould, page 87

June's Chocolate Trifle, page 86

Golden Squares,
page 83

Uncle Ian's Special Apple Roll Slices,
page 81

Angela's Cornish Custard Pie,
page 79

Bakewell Tart, page 82

Channel Island Plum Tart, page 81

Almond Date Flan, page 79

Standard Kinds Assorted *Breakfast Biscuits*

An Essential War-time Food

made by

Huntley & Palmers

The World-Famous Biscuit Manufacturers

Teatime is a uniquely British institution – and one we should be proud of. Cake, bread and biscuit making is an art – eating the result, an enjoyable experience.

Today we take the easy availability of eggs, cooking fat and sugar for granted. You would think that when they were scarce, such as in wartime, cake and biscuit making would come to a halt. But no, the British housewife responded to the challenge and devised deliciously ingenious substitutes. The cakes, biscuits and breads of this period have a charm all their own – they're interesting and inexpensive to make, and mouth watering to eat.

SISTER LIZ'S DATE FINGERS

Makes 18

2 oz margarine
1 rounded tablespoon golden syrup
3 oz stoned dates
½ teaspoon almond flavouring
4 oz barley flakes or rolled oats
2 oz self-raising flour

Preheat the oven to 350°F, Gas Mark 4. Grease an 8 inch square cake tin.

Place the margarine and syrup in a saucepan, and heat gently until the margarine has melted. Chop the dates and stir in with the almond flavouring. Mix the barley flakes or rolled oats with the flour and stir into the ingredients in the pan. Press into the prepared tin with damp fingers until the mixture is pressed down smoothly and about $\frac{1}{3}$ inch in thickness. Bake in the centre of the preheated oven for 20 to 25 minutes. Leave in the tin for a few minutes to set and, while still warm, cut into fingers. Remove from the tin when cold.

SPICED OAT COOKIES

Makes 24

2 oz plain flour
4 oz rolled oats
3 oz castor sugar
¼ level teaspoon bicarbonate of soda
½ teaspoon mixed spice
¼ teaspoon nutmeg
3 oz margarine
1 tablespoon boiling water

Mix together the flour, rolled oats, sugar, bicarbonate of soda and the spices. Melt the margarine, add the water and mix into the dry ingredients to form a firm dough. Turn out on to a lightly floured surface, form into a roll, about $2\frac{1}{4}$ inches in diameter, wrap in greaseproof paper and chill.

Preheat the oven to 400°F, Gas Mark 6. Grease a baking tray.

Cut the roll into thin slices and lay them on the baking tray. Bake in the preheated oven for about 12 minutes or until the biscuits are lightly browned; cool on a wire rack.

THAR CAKES

Makes about 18

5 oz fine or medium oatmeal
3 oz plain flour
½ oz sugar
1 level teaspoon ground ginger
1 oz mixed cut peel, optional
¼ level teaspoon bicarbonate of soda
1½ oz butter or margarine
4 level tablespoons golden syrup

Preheat the oven to 350°F, Gas Mark 4. Grease a baking tray.

Mix the oatmeal, flour, sugar, ginger, peel if used, and bicarbonate of soda together in a basin.

In a saucepan over a low heat, melt the butter or margarine and syrup and then stir in the dry ingredients. Allow to cool slightly.

Knead the mixture together until smooth, and roll out on a lightly floured surface to $\frac{1}{4}$ inch thickness. Cut into rounds with a $2\frac{1}{2}$ inch cutter. Place on the baking tray and bake in the centre of the preheated oven for about 8 minutes, or until golden brown.

NAN'S ORANGE BREAD

6 oz self-raising flour
3 oz castor sugar
1 egg
Grated rind of 1 orange
1 rounded tablespoon orange marmalade
4 tablespoons milk
1 oz margarine
Slices of fresh orange to decorate

Preheat the oven to 375°F, Gas Mark 5. Grease and line the bottom of a 1 lb loaf tin.

Place the flour and sugar in a mixing bowl. Beat the egg and mix in the orange rind, marmalade and milk. Melt the margarine and pour into the egg mixture. Pour into the flour and sugar and mix lightly together.

Place the mixture into the prepared tin, arrange the orange slices on top to decorate and bake in the centre of the oven for $1\frac{1}{4}$ to $1\frac{1}{2}$ hours.

Turn out and cool on a wire rack. Serve in slices spread with butter or marmalade.

POTATO SCONES

Makes 18

1 lb potatoes
4 oz plain flour
1 level teaspoon salt
2 level teaspoons baking powder
2 oz margarine
Milk for mixing

Peel the potatoes, and cook in boiling water until tender; drain well and mash.

Preheat the oven to 425°F, Gas Mark 7. Grease a baking tray. Sift the flour, salt and baking powder into a mixing bowl. Rub in the margarine until the mixture resembles fine breadcrumbs. Add the mashed potato and mix well. Add enough milk to make a soft, but not sticky, dough. Knead gently on a lightly floured surface until smooth. Roll out to a $\frac{3}{4}$ inch thickness circle, and cut into triangles or 2 inch rounds. Place on the baking tray and bake near the top of the preheated oven for about 15 minutes.

TANGY SAVOURY BISCUITS

Makes 25 to 30

Here's a good way of using up a small piece of hard cheese.

6 oz plain flour
1 level teaspoon celery salt
¼ teaspoon cayenne pepper
3 oz margarine
3 oz cheese, finely grated

Preheat the oven to 400°F, Gas Mark 6.

Place the flour, celery salt and cayenne pepper in a mixing bowl. Rub in the margarine until the mixture resembles fine breadcrumbs. Stir in the grated cheese then mix to a firm dough with about 2 tablespoons of water. Knead lightly until smooth on a lightly floured surface, then roll out the dough to $\frac{1}{4}$ inch thickness, and cut into rounds with a 2 inch cutter.

Place the biscuits on baking trays and prick lightly with a fork. Bake in the centre and one shelf above the centre of the preheated oven for about 15 minutes.

HONEY SCONES

Makes about 10

4 oz plain flour
1 level tablespoon baking powder
Pinch of salt
4 oz wholemeal flour
2 oz margarine
3 level tablespoons honey
¼ pint milk

Preheat the oven to 450°F, Gas Mark 8. Grease a baking tray.

Sift together the plain flour, baking powder and salt in a mixing bowl, then stir in the wholemeal flour. Rub in the margarine until the mixture resembles fine breadcrumbs. Add the honey and enough of the milk, to make a fairly soft, but not sticky, dough. Knead very gently on a lightly floured surface (do not overknead or you will toughen the dough).

Roll out to ¾ inch thickness and cut into rounds with a 2 inch cutter. Place on the baking tray, brush the tops with a little milk and bake in the preheated oven for 10 to 15 minutes, until well risen and golden. Cool on a wire rack.

OATMEAL AND CHEESE BISCUITS

Makes about 20 biscuits

4 oz self-raising flour
4 oz oatmeal
¼ teaspoon salt
2 oz margarine
2 oz cooking fat
2 oz cheese

Preheat the oven to 400°F, Gas Mark 6. Grease two baking trays.

Mix together the flour, oatmeal and salt in a mixing bowl. Rub in the margarine and the cooking fat until the mixture resembles fine breadcrumbs. Grate the cheese and stir in. Mix to a firm dough with about 4 tablespoons of water.

Roll out on a lightly floured surface to $\frac{1}{4}$ inch thickness and cut into rounds with a $2\frac{1}{2}$ inch round cutter. Bake in the centre and one shelf above the centre of the preheated oven for about 10 minutes. Cool on a wire rack.

CHOCOLATE FUDGE CAKES

Makes 8 wedges

1 (6.17 oz) packet shortcake biscuits
3 oz margarine
2 oz sugar
2 level tablespoons golden syrup
3 level tablespoons cocoa
1 small bar plain chocolate

Grease a 7 inch fluted flan ring or shallow cake tin; place the flan ring on a plate if used.

Crush the biscuits. Place the margarine, sugar and golden syrup in a small pan, and heat gently until the margarine has melted.

Stir in the cocoa and the biscuit crumbs. Press the mixture into the flan ring or cake tin and leave in a very cold place to set. Remove the flan ring, if used.

Melt the chocolate in a small basin set over a pan of hot water. Spread the chocolate over the top of the cake and set to chill, again, then cut into wedges.

PANCAKE SCONES

Makes about 15

To cook these scones have ready a griddle or heavy-based frying pan, greased and hot.

4 oz plain flour
½ level teaspoon bicarbonate of soda
1 level teaspoon cream of tartar
½ level teaspoon salt
½ oz margarine
1 egg
2 teaspoons golden syrup
3 fluid oz milk

Sift the flour, bicarbonate of soda, cream of tartar and salt into a mixing bowl and rub in the margarine until the mixture resembles fine breadcrumbs.

Separate the egg and mix the yolk with the syrup. Beat into the flour mixture with the milk until smooth and like thick cream. Whisk the egg white until stiff and then fold into the batter.

Drop spoonfuls of the mixture on to the prepared griddle or heavy-based frying pan, and cook, turning once the bubbles have burst, until golden brown on both sides. Serve hot with butter.

BROWN SODA BREAD

Makes 1 round loaf

If you have any buttermilk, use it instead of milk for mixing as it helps to give a lighter dough. This is a quick bread to make without yeast.

½ lb plain flour
½ lb wholewheat flour
1 level teaspoon bicarbonate of soda
1 level teaspoon cream of tartar
1 level teaspoon salt
1 level tablespoon golden syrup
About ½ pint milk

Preheat the oven to 400°F, Gas Mark 6.

Mix together the flours, bicarbonate of soda, cream of tartar and salt in a mixing bowl. Add the golden syrup and enough of the milk to mix lightly to a soft, but not sticky dough. Knead very lightly, about 10 times, on a lightly floured surface; do not over-knead or you will toughen the dough, and shape into a round about 2 inches thick. Mark a cross in the middle and bake in the preheated oven for about 25 to 30 minutes, or until the bread sounds hollow when tapped underneath. Serve fresh and warm.

CRUMB FUDGE

Makes 12 wedges

2 tablespoons syrup
2 oz margarine
2 oz sugar
2 oz cocoa
Few drops vanilla, peppermint or orange essence
4 oz browned breadcrumbs (see page 65)

Grease a 7 inch sandwich tin.

Heat the syrup, margarine, sugar and cocoa gently until the margarine is melted. Stir in the required flavouring and then the bread-crumbs. Mix thoroughly and press into the prepared sandwich tin; spread evenly and mark lightly into wedges.

Leave for 24 hours. This fudge improves with keeping for a day or two.

WINE BISCUITS

Makes 45

Instead of grated orange rind, try the same amount of very finely chopped candied peel.

4 oz margarine
9 oz plain flour
5 oz castor sugar
1 egg
2 tablespoons milk
Grated rind of one small orange
1 level teaspoon caraway seeds

Preheat the oven to 450°F, Gas Mark 8. Grease two baking trays.

Rub the margarine into the flour until the mixture resembles fine breadcrumbs. Stir in the sugar. Beat the egg and the milk together and stir this, a little at a time, into the dry ingredients to make a firm dough. Divide the dough in half. Work the grated orange rind into one half and the caraway seeds into the other.

Roll out one half of the dough on a lightly floured surface to about ¼ inch thickness and cut into rounds with a 2 inch cutter. Repeat with the other piece of dough. Place the bisuits on to the baking trays. Bakes in the preheated oven for 5 to 10 minutes, but watch them carefully because they burn easily. Cool on a wire rack to become crisp.

SHORTAGE TIME SHORT CAKE

This is nothing like shortbread, but is a kind of cake, delicious when filled with jam, stewed fruit or, if being really extravagant, with crushed raspberries or strawberries and cream.

8 oz plain flour
2 level teaspoons baking powder
2 oz margarine
1 tablespoon sugar
1 egg
3 fluid oz milk
Jam or fruit

Preheat the oven to 400°F, Gas Mark 6. Grease two 7 inch sandwich tins.

Sift the flour and baking powder together into a mixing bowl and then rub in the margarine until the mixture resembles fine breadcrumbs. Mix in the sugar.

Beat the egg lightly and add to the fat and flour mixture with sufficient milk to make a soft, but not sticky dough.

Knead the dough very lightly on a lightly floured surface and divide into two equal-sized pieces. Roll each half into a 7 inch circle. Place each of the rounds into the prepared tins and bake in the centre of the preheated oven for 15 to 20 minutes or until risen and golden. Turn out and cool on a wire rack.

When the cake is cool enough, fill with jam, stewed or fresh fruit.

APPLE CHEESE CAKES

Makes about 17

6 oz shortcrust pastry (see page 65)
1 lb cooking apples
2 cloves
3 oz brown sugar
1 oz butter
2 eggs
Lemon flavoured glacé icing

Preheat the oven to 375°F, Gas Mark 5. Roll out the pastry on a lightly floured surface and cut into 3½ inch rounds and line small patty tins.

Peel, core and chop the apples. Put them into a pan with 3 tablespoons of water and the cloves; stew gently until soft. Remove the cloves, then rub the apples through a sieve or liquidise. Return to the pan, add the sugar and butter and stir until dissolved; remove from the heat. Beat the eggs and mix in to the apples. Pour the mixture into a jug and pour into the pastry cases to almost fill them. Bake in the preheated oven for 30 to 35 minutes. Turn out and cool on a wire rack and decorate with a lemon flavoured glacé icing.

COUSIN AVRIL'S EGGLESS CAKE

7 oz plain flour
2 oz cornflour
½ teaspoon mixed spice
4 oz margarine
4 oz sultanas
4 oz currants
2 oz chopped mixed peel
4 oz brown sugar
½ level teaspoon bicarbonate of soda
8 tablespoons milk
½ teaspoon vinegar

Preheat the oven to 325°F, Gas Mark 3. Grease and line the bottom of a deep 6½ inch round cake tin.

Sift the flour, cornflour and spice together in a mixing bowl. Rub in the margarine until the mixture resembles fine breadcrumbs. Mix in the dried fruit, mixed peel and sugar.

Dissolve the bicarbonate of soda in 1 table-spoon of the milk. Add the vinegar and the dissolved soda to the cake mixture. Fold in 7 tablespoons of milk.

Place the mixture into the prepared cake tin, smooth the top and bake in the centre of the preheated oven for 1½ to 1¾ hours. Leave to cool in the tin for a few minutes, then turn out on to a wire rack and leave to cool completely.

OATMEAL COOKIES

Makes about 25

8 oz rolled oats
4 oz castor sugar
Pinch of salt
3 oz margarine
2 rounded tablespoons golden syrup
1 level teaspoon baking powder
1 teaspoon almond flavouring
Milk

Preheat the oven to 375°F, Gas Mark 5. Grease two baking trays.

Mix together the oats, sugar and salt in a mixing bowl. In a small saucepan over a low heat melt the margarine until it is liquid. Add the syrup and baking powder and beat well. Stir in the almond flavouring then pour into the dry ingredients. Mix together until the mixture is well blended and there are no dry oats left. Drop spoonfuls of the mixture on to the baking trays leaving plenty of space around each. Pat the cookies down with the back of a wooden spoon dipped in milk.

Bake in the centre and one shelf above the centre of the preheated oven for about 10 minutes. When they are cooked leave to cool on the tray for a few minutes then lift each biscuit from the tray and leave to cool on a wire rack.

AUNTIE JOYCE'S HOLIDAY CAKE

A good cake to have on hand during the school holidays to answer those calls between-meals of 'I'm hungry, what can I have to eat?'

12 oz plain flour
3 oz castor sugar
½ level teaspoon mixed spice
4 oz margarine
8 oz dried fruit
2 fluid oz milk
1 teaspoon almond flavouring
1 rounded tablespoon golden syrup or orange marmalade
1 level teaspoon bicarbonate of soda

Preheat the oven to 325°F, Gas Mark 3. Grease and line the bottom of a deep, 8 inch round cake tin.

Mix the flour, sugar and mixed spice in a mixing bowl. Place the margarine, fruit and 8 fluid ounces of water into a saucepan and heat gently until the margarine has melted. Bring the mixture to the boil and boil for 5 minutes. Remove the saucepan from the heat and allow the contents to cool a little. Stir in the milk, almond flavouring, golden syrup or marmalade and the bicarbonate of soda. When the soda froths up, pour the mixture into the flour and sugar mixture. Gently stir together until all the ingredients are well blended.

Place the mixture into the prepared cake tin, smooth the top and bake in the centre of the preheated oven for about 1½ hours. Leave to cool in the tin for a few minutes then turn out on to a wire rack and leave until completely cooled.

CARAWAY SEED CAKE

Most seed cakes tend to go dry – but this one shouldn't. The syrup and the slow cooking, which gives a smooth, soft texture right through, with no hard crust on the outside, both help to keep it moist.

3 oz margarine
4 oz castor sugar
1 rounded tablespoon golden syrup
2 eggs
6 oz plain flour
4 fluid oz milk
¼ to ½ oz caraway seeds (according to taste)
Sugar for sprinkling

Preheat the oven to 325°F, Gas Mark 3. Grease and line the bottom of a deep, 6 inch round cake tin.

Cream the margarine and sugar together in a mixing bowl until light and fluffy and then beat in the golden syrup. Beat the eggs then add them, gradually, to the margarine and sugar mixture, beating each addition well before adding more. Sift the flour and fold in, half at a time with the milk, until thoroughly blended, then stir in the caraway seeds. The mixture should be a soft, dropping consistency.

Place the mixture into the prepared cake tin, smooth the top and then make a small hollow in the centre. Sprinkle a little sugar over the top then bake in the preheated oven for $1\frac{1}{4}$ to $1\frac{1}{2}$ hours. Turn out and cool on a wire rack.

TEACUP APPLE SAUCE CAKE

You will need a teacupful of apple sauce for this recipe. Peel and core the apples and cook them slowly in a saucepan with a little water. When tender rub through a sieve or liquidise. Do not sweeten. A standard teacup should hold about 6 to 7 fluid ounces. If yours aren't exactly this size, don't worry, as long as you use the same cup for measuring all the ingredients.

1 teacup castor sugar
½ teacup margarine
1 level teaspoon ground cloves
¼ level teaspoon nutmeg
¼ level teaspoon cinnamon
1 teacup raisins
1 teaspoon bicarbonate of soda
1 teacup apple sauce
2 teacups plain flour
Apple slices, to decorate

Preheat the oven to 350°F, Gas Mark 4. Grease a 1 lb loaf tin.

Cream together the sugar and the margarine, until well mixed. Add the ground cloves, nutmeg, cinnamon and raisins and mix well.

Dissolve the bicarbonate of soda in 1 teaspoon of water, then stir it into the apple sauce. When this mixture foams up, add it to the other mixed ingredients and beat well together. Finally, sift the flour and fold in half at a time.

Place the mixture into the prepared tin, place a few apple slices on top to decorate, and bake in the centre of the preheated oven for about $1\frac{1}{2}$ to $1\frac{3}{4}$ hours. Leave to cool in the tin for a few minutes, then turn out on to a wire rack and leave to cool completely.

SLY CAKES

Makes 12

You will need 8 oz of prepared shortcrust pastry for these strangely named cakes with a lovely moist filling.

1 level teaspoon cornflour
¼ pint water
4 oz seedless raisins or sultanas
2 oz currants
2 tablespoons brown sugar
½ teaspoon mixed spice
8 oz shortcrust pastry (see page 65)
Sugar for sprinkling

Preheat the oven to 400°F, Gas Mark 6.

Mix the cornflour smoothly with a little of the water. Put the remainder of the water into a saucepan with the raisins or sultanas and currants.

Bring to the boil then simmer gently until the water is almost absorbed, then add the blended cornflour and stir until the mixture thickens. Stir in the sugar and spice and leave to cool.

Divide the pastry into two equal pieces. Roll out one half on a lightly floured surface to a rectangle 8 inches by 12 inches. Place on a baking tray. Spread the currant and sultana mixture evenly over the pastry to within ½ inch of the edges. Roll out the other piece of pastry to the same size, dampen the edges, and place on top; press the edges well together with the back of a fork to seal. Mark the top into 12 rectangles with the back of a knife. Brush over with water, then sprinkle with sugar.

Place in the preheated oven and bake for about 30 minutes, or until golden brown. Place on a wire rack and cut into squares when cold.

MOIST CARROT DATE CAKE

During the war people were encouraged to eat carrots to help them resist infection and enable them to see better in the dark. Whether this is true or not, the sweetness of carrots does make it possible to use them to replace part of the sugar in puddings and cakes, and to give this cake in particular its special moist quality.

½ lb carrots
6 oz stoned dates
4 oz castor sugar
2 oz margarine
2 oz cooking fat
1 teaspoon vanilla flavouring
2 eggs
1 level teaspoon bicarbonate of soda
12 oz self-raising flour
1 level teaspoon cinnamon
7 tablespoons milk
Halved dates to decorate

Preheat the oven to 350°F, Gas Mark 4. Grease and line the bottom of a deep 7 inch square cake tin.

Peel and finely grate the carrots. Chop the dates. Cream the sugar, margarine and cooking fat together until light and fluffy. Beat in the grated carrot and vanilla. In another bowl beat the eggs up well with the bicarbonate of soda.

Beat the eggs into the creamed mixture, gradually, then stir in the dates. Sift the flour and fold into the mixture with the cinnamon, a little at a time. Stir in enough of the milk to give a soft dropping consistency.

Place the mixture into the cake tin, smooth the top and bake in the centre of the preheated oven for 1½ to 1¾ hours. Turn out and cool on a wire rack. Decorate the top of the cake with halved dates and serve cut into squares.

Michael's favourite lemon cake

The topping (cooked in): 2 oz plain flour,
2 oz margarine, 1 tablespoon brown sugar,
2 tablespoons lemon curd.
The cake: 4 oz margarine, 4 oz caster sugar, 2 eggs,
8 oz self-raising flour, grated rind & juice of one
lemon.

Oven on at 350 F, Gas 4. Grease & line bottom
of deep, 8 inch round cake tin. To make topping:
flour and margarine — rub in, then add sugar and
lemon curd.
For cake: cream marg and sugar, beat till fluffy.
Beat in eggs one at a time. Sift half the flour
and fold in.
Add lemon juice and rind and fold in with
rest of flour.
Place mixture in tin and smooth top.

Carefully spread topping all over
uncooked cake.

Bake in the centre of oven for 40 mins.

Leave to cool in tin for a few mins,
turn out on wire rack to cool
completely.

WHEATMEAL BREAD

Makes one 2 lb loaf or two 1 lb loaves

1 oz fresh yeast or 1 level tablespoon dried yeast and 1 level
teaspoon castor sugar
¾ pint warm water
1½ lb wholewheat flour
1 level tablespoon salt
1 level tablespoon castor sugar
1 oz margarine

Gease one 2 lb loaf tin or two 1 lb loaf tins.

Mix the fresh yeast with ¼ pint of the warm water. (If using dried yeast dissolve 1 level teaspoon of sugar in ¼ pint of warm water and sprinkle over the dried yeast. Leave until frothy.)

Place the flour, salt and 1 level tablespoon castor sugar in a large mixing bowl; rub in the margarine. Stir in the yeast liquid with enough of the remaining water to give a soft dough. Knead well on a lightly floured surface until the dough is smooth and no longer sticky, about 5 to 10 minutes. Place the dough in a lightly floured mixing bowl, cover with cling wrap and leave in a warm place to rise until the dough has doubled in size.

Re-knead the dough to knock it back to its original size, and beat with your fist to knock out any air bubbles. Roll up the dough like a Swiss roll and tuck under the ends so that it fits the 2 lb loaf tin. (For two loaves, divide the dough in half, shape and fit into two 1 lb loaf tins.) Brush the top of the bread with a little oil.

Cover the tin or tins with cling wrap and leave in a warm place until the dough has risen to the top of the tins. Preheat the oven to 450°F, Gas Mark 8.

Brush the bread with a little milk and bake in the preheated oven for 30 to 40 minutes for a 2 lb loaf, or 25 to 30 minutes for the 1 lb loaves, or until the bread sounds hollow when tapped underneath. Turn out and cool on a wire rack.

GOLDEN BREAD

In days of shortages, this was served oven-hot for tea. Butter, though expensive, is always available these days, so for an extra special treat, cut this cake into slices whilst warm and spread with butter.

6 oz self-raising flour
3 oz margarine
1 oz walnuts
2 oz sultanas
3 oz browned breadcrumbs (see page 65)
1 egg
4 tablespoons milk
3 level tablespoons golden syrup

Preheat the oven to 350°F, Gas Mark 4. Grease a 2 lb loaf tin.

Sift the flour into a mixing bowl and then rub in the margarine until the mixture resembles fine breadcrumbs. Chop the walnuts and lightly dust the sultanas in a little flour. Add the walnuts, sultanas and breadcrumbs to the flour mixture and mix well.

In another basin beat the egg and then mix in the milk and golden syrup. Pour the egg mixture into the flour mixture and stir lightly together. Place the mixture into the prepared tin, smooth the top and bake in the centre of the preheated oven for about 45 minutes. Turn out and cool on a wire rack.

MRS GUY'S WARTIME BARM LOAF

8 oz self-raising flour
Pinch of salt
4 oz dried fruit
¼ pint milk
2 rounded tablespoons orange marmalade
2 level tablespoons golden syrup

Preheat the oven to 350°F, Gas Mark 4. Grease and line the bottom of a 1 lb loaf tin.

Place, the flour, salt, and fruit into a mixing bowl. Mix the milk with the marmalade and golden syrup. Pour into the flour and mix lightly together. Place the mixture into the prepared loaf tin and bake in the centre of the preheated oven for about 40 minutes. Turn out and cool on a wire rack and brush the top with a little golden syrup.

MARMALADE CAKE

When sugar was difficult to obtain the 1940's housewife had to find a substitute. In this cake golden syrup is used instead. Incidentally it's at its most delicious when eaten warm straight from the oven, so bake it just before teatime. Serve it spread with butter.

8 oz self-raising flour
3 oz margarine
1 egg
¼ pint milk
3 level tablespoons golden syrup
2 rounded tablespoons marmalade

Preheat the oven to 325°F, Gas Mark 3. Grease and line the bottom of a deep 7 inch square cake tin.

Sift the flour into a mixing bowl and rub in the margarine until the mixture resembles fine breadcrumbs. Beat the egg in a basin and mix in the milk, golden syrup and marmalade. Stir this mixture lightly into the flour. Pour into the prepared cake tin and bake in the centre of the preheated oven for about 1 hour. Turn out and cool on a wire rack.

CHOCOLATE SHORTBREAD BISCUITS

Makes about 40

5 oz butter or margarine
3 oz castor sugar
1 egg
¼ teaspoon vanilla flavouring
7 oz plain flour
1 oz cornflour
1 oz cocoa powder
Milk
Castor sugar for sprinkling

Preheat the oven to 350°F, Gas Mark 4.

Cream together the butter or margarine and the sugar. Beat in the egg and the vanilla. Sift together the flour, cornflour and cocoa and mix into the creamed mixture to form a firm dough. Knead together until smooth, wrap in greaseproof paper and leave in the refrigerator for about half an hour to become firm.

Roll out on a lightly floured surface and cut into rounds with a 2 inch cutter. Place the biscuits on baking trays, prick lightly with a fork, then brush each one with a little milk and sprinkle on a little sugar.

Bake in the centre of the preheated oven for about 20 minutes. Cool on a wire rack.

SYRUP SPONGE CAKE

2 oz cooking fat
2 rounded tablespoons golden syrup
¼ pint milk
8 oz plain flour
2 oz sultanas
1 level teaspoon baking powder
3 oz castor sugar
1 level teaspoon bicarbonate of soda
2 teaspoons ground ginger

Preheat the oven to 375°F, Gas Mark 5. Grease and line the bottom of a deep, 7 inch round cake tin.

Place the cooking fat, golden syrup and milk in a large saucepan. Bring to the boil, remove from the heat and allow to cool. Stir in the remaining ingredients, mixing well. Place the mixture in the prepared tin and bake in the centre of the preheated oven for 30 to 45 minutes. Turn out and cool on a wire rack.

SUGAR CRISPS

Makes about 40

This biscuit dough needs to 'rest' in the refrigerator before baking. If ginger is not your favourite spice, try powdered cinnamon instead.

3 oz margarine
5 oz castor sugar
1 egg
8 oz plain flour
1 level teaspoon ground ginger

Cream together the margarine and the sugar until well mixed. Beat the egg and beat into the creamed mixture. Sift together the flour and ginger and stir into the creamed mixture to mix to a firm dough.

Knead the dough on a lightly floured surface until smooth, form into a roll about 1½ inches in diameter. Wrap it in a piece of greaseproof paper and leave it in the refrigerator for a couple of hours before baking.

Preheat the oven to 375°F, Gas Mark 5. Grease two baking trays.

Cut the roll into thin slices and lay them on the baking trays leaving about ¼ inch spare between each. Bake in the centre and one shelf above the centre of the preheated oven for about 10 minutes or until they are pale golden brown.

FARLS (OATMEAL SCONES)

Makes 8

6 oz self-raising flour
½ level teaspoon salt
1 oz margarine
2 oz oatmeal
Just under ½ pint milk

Preheat the oven to 425°F, Gas Mark 7. Grease a baking tray.

Place the flour in a mixing bowl with the salt. Rub in the margarine until the mixture resembles fine breadcrumbs. Add the oatmeal and mix to a soft, but not sticky dough, with the milk. Roll out on a lightly floured surface to a circle of ¾ inch thickness, and cut into 8 triangular shapes. Place on the baking tray and bake near the top of the preheated oven for 15 minutes or until golden brown.

and the egg, into the dry ingredients and lightly beat until smooth.

Pour the mixture into the prepared tin and bake in the centre of the preheated oven for 30 to 40 minutes. Leave in the tin, and when cold cut into squares.

PEANUT BUTTER FRUIT CAKE

In this cake peanut butter is used instead of fat – you'll find it takes longer to cream than margarine because it is stiffer and stickier.

4 oz peanut butter
3 oz soft brown sugar
4 oz sultanas
8 oz plain flour
½ level teaspoon mixed spices
9 fluid oz milk
1 level tablespoon black treacle or golden syrup
½ level teaspoon bicarbonate of soda

Preheat the oven to 325°F, Gas Mark 3. Grease and line the bottom of a deep, 7 inch round cake tin.

Cream the peanut butter and sugar together with a wooden spoon until well mixed. Stir in the fruit. Sift the flour and spice into another bowl. Warm the milk, then mix in the black treacle or syrup and the bicarbonate of soda. Fold in the flour mixture and the milk mixture alternately, a little at a time, to the creamed mixture, to make a soft dropping consistency.

Place the mixture into the prepared tin, smooth the top and bake in the centre of the prehated oven for 1½ to 2 hours. (Cover with a piece of foil to protect the top if it begins to get too brown.) Turn out and leave to cool on a wire rack.

LIGHT FRUITY GINGERBREAD

Makes 18 squares

Use a shallow tin for baking this gingerbread.

8 oz plain flour
2 level teaspoons ground ginger
½ level teaspoon mixed spice
3 oz sultanas
2 oz soft brown sugar
1 egg
8 level tablespoons golden syrup
4 oz lard
¼ pint milk
1 level teaspoon bicarbonate of soda

Preheat the oven to 350°F, Gas Mark 4. Grease a shallow tin, 7 inches by 10 inches.

Sift the flour and the spices into a mixing bowl. Add the sultanas and sugar. Beat the egg. Measure the syrup into a saucepan, add the lard and heat through until the lard has melted. Warm the milk and stir in the bicarbonate of soda.

Pour the syrup mixture, the milk mixture,

OATMEAL WELSH CAKES

Makes about 18

4 oz plain flour
¼ teaspoon salt
2 level teaspoons baking powder
4 oz medium oatmeal
2 oz sugar
2 oz margarine
Pinch of grated nutmeg
2 oz currants
2 to 3 tablespoons milk

Sift together the flour, salt and the baking powder and add the oatmeal and sugar. Rub in the margarine until the mixture resembles fine breadcrumbs. Add the nutmeg and the currants and mix to a firm dough with the milk. Roll out to about ¼ inch thickness, and cut into rounds with a 2½ inch cutter. Cook for about 5 minutes on a lightly greased hot griddle or in a greased heavy-based frying pan, turning once until brown on both sides.

BREAKFAST BANNOCKS

Makes about 12

6 oz plain flour
2 oz wheatmeal flour
½ teaspoon salt
2 level teaspoons baking powder
1 oz margarine
2 teaspoons sugar
¼ pint milk

Mix together the flours, salt and baking powder in a mixing bowl. Rub in the margarine until the mixture resembles fine breadcrumbs; add the sugar. Make a well in the centre and mix in the milk to form a soft, not sticky dough. Roll out on a lightly floured surface, to ¼ inch thickness, and cut into rounds with a 2 inch cutter. Place on a well greased hot griddle or in a greased heavy-based frying pan. Reduce the heat and cook, turning once, until well risen and brown.

LEMON CURD KNOBS

Makes about 15

7 oz self-raising flour
2 oz margarine
2 oz sugar
1 oz fine semolina
1 egg
4 drops lemon flavouring
4 tablespoons milk
Lemon curd

Preheat the oven to 350°F, Gas Mark 4. Grease 2 baking trays.

Sift the flour into a mixing bowl and rub in the margarine until the mixture resembles fine breadcrumbs. Stir in the sugar and the semolina.

Beat the egg lightly and add the lemon flavouring. Add the egg to the dry ingredients with the milk to make a fairly firm dough.

Roll the dough into small even-sized balls in the palms of your hands. With the handle of a floured wooden spoon, make a fairly large hole in the centre of each. Put a very small amount of lemon curd into this hole, then squeeze the dough together over the top so that the lemon curd will stay inside the cakes. Brush over each cake with a little milk and place on the baking trays. Bake in the centre of the preheated oven for 20 to 25 minutes.

JAMS, JELLIES AND CHUTNEYS

Making jams, jellies and chutneys brings out the squirrel instinct in people. Using fruit, in season, that you've probably picked yourself, preparing it, boiling it up (with the accompanying delicious smells), then potting it in warm, sparkling jars and finally storing it away – what could be more satisfying. You can actually see the results of what you've done for several months – unlike everyday cooking which gets eaten up in no time.

Making your own preserves is also economical if you gather fruit for free – like blackberries and elderberries – from the hedgerows.

For the 30s and 40s cook jam, jelly and chutney making was (with bottling) the only way of preserving, rather than wasting, a bounteous crop of rhubarb, apple and so on. The days of the home freezer ready to receive the seasonal surplus, polythene bagged, had yet to come.

RHUBARB JAM

This jam has a rich flavour and is good used in tarts.

3 lb rhubarb
1 lb seedless or stoned raisins
2 lb sugar
Juice of 2 lemons

Wipe the rhubarb and chop it into 1-inch squares.

Wash the raisins and chop finely.

Put the rhubarb into the pan and cook very slowly over a low heat until the juices begin to run. Turn up the heat and simmer until it is soft. Add the sugar, raisins and lemon juice.

Stir to dissolve the sugar, then bring slowly to the boil. Boil fast for 30 to 35 minutes, or until setting point is reached. Pot and seal while hot.

CARROT MARMALADE

1 lb carrots
4 medium sized lemons
2¾ pints of water
4 lb sugar

Peel and grate the carrots.

Grate the lemon rind. Squeeze the juice from the lemons.

Put the grated carrots, lemon rind and juice in the pan and add the water. Boil all together for three quarters of an hour.

Add the sugar and stir well to dissolve, then boil for a further 20 or 30 minutes, or until setting point is reached.

APPLE GINGER

A beautifully amber coloured jam.

4 lb apples
1 pint water
1 teaspoon ground ginger
4 tablespoons ginger syrup
3 lb sugar
4 oz preserved ginger

Peel, core and slice the apples. Tie the peel and cores in a square of muslin. Place the apples, water, ground ginger and ginger syrup in a pan. Add the bag of peel and cores and simmer gently until tender.

Remove the bag of peel and cores, squeezing all the juice from it into the pan. Mash the apples with a wooden spoon.

Chop the preserved ginger and add with the sugar to the pan of apple. Cook slowly, stirring continuously until the sugar is dissolved, then boil until setting point is reached. Pot in warm jars and seal.

DRIED APRICOT JAM

1 lb dried apricots
3 pints of water
3 lb sugar
Juice of 1 lemon

Wash and dry the apricots. For a very smooth jam you can mince them. For a medium-textured jam, cut the apricots into pieces and for a fruity jam leave them whole.

Put the prepared apricots in a large bowl, cover with the water and leave to soak for 24 hours.

Put the contents of the bowl into a pan and simmer gently for about 30 minutes. Add the sugar and the fresh lemon juice. Stir over a low heat to dissolve the sugar, then bring to the boil.

Boil moderately fast for about 25 to 30 minutes, or until setting point is reached. Pot while hot, but leave until absolutely cold before sealing.

APPLE ORANGE JELLY

2 lb apples
½ pint water
2 oranges
Sugar

Do not core or peel the apples but just cut them up. Put the chopped fruit into the pan with the water.

Finely grate the orange peel and squeeze out the juice. Add the grated peel and juice to the apples.

Simmer the contents of the pan over a low heat until the apple is soft and pulpy. Remove from the heat and then place the contents in a scalded jelly bag. Leave to drip until all the juice has come through. You can squeeze the bag gently to remove the last drops.

Measure the amount of juice. For each pint you will need 14 oz of sugar. Put the juice and sugar into the pan and stir well. Bring to the boil, then boil fast until setting point is reached.

Pot into small jars and put waxed paper circles on top. Seal well when the jelly is absolutely cold.

BRAMBLE JELLY - made at home

. . . is good to eat

with Hovis and butter

for tea.

ELDERBERRY AND APPLE JAM

In this recipe the apples are not cooked with the elderberries, for if they were they would go leathery, rather than soft and pulpy.

3 lb elderberries
2 lb apples
4 lb sugar

To clean the elderberries, shake them in bunches in warm water. Remove the stalks and put the fruit into the pan. Cook over a very low heat until the juices begin to run, then simmer gently for 30 minutes.

Core and peel the apples and cut into slices or small pieces. Cook over a low heat, with just sufficient water to prevent burning, until they are soft and pulpy. For a smooth jam you can pass the apples through a sieve. For a chunkier jam, use them as they are.

Stir the apple into the elderberries. Add the sugar and leave for 15 minutes for it to dissolve. Bring the mixture to the boil and then boil quickly until setting point is reached. Setting point will be reached fairly quickly, so test frequently. Pot and seal while hot.

BRAMBLE JELLY

4 lb blackberries
1 lb apples
½ pint water
Sugar

Pick over the blackberries, removing any stalks and leaves. Wash the apples. Cut them into pieces without peeling or coring.

Put the blackberries, apples and water into a preserving pan and boil until they are pulpy.

Place the fruit pulp in a scalded jelly bag and leave to drip for 12 hours.

Measure the juice carefully and allow 1 lb of sugar to each pint of juice.

Place the sugar and juice in a pan and cook over a low heat, stirring continuously, until the sugar is dissolved. Boil for 10 to 15 minutes or until setting point is reached.

Skim, then pour into small, warmed jars and cover at once.

MINT JELLY

You can use either gooseberries or apples for this jelly, they both give a good firm set. The apples should be weighed when they are cored and cut up into small pieces.

2 lb gooseberries or apples
Sugar
18 or more stems of young, fresh mint
4 tablespoons finely chopped mint

If using apples, core them and cut up into small pieces. If using gooseberries, top and tail them.

Put the fruit into the pan, adding just enough water to cover the bottom of the pan. Simmer over a low heat until the juices begin to run and then cook gently until the fruit is soft and pulpy.

Put the fruit into a scalded jelly bag and allow to drip through. Squeeze the bag very gently to remove the last drops of juice.

Measure the juice, and for each pint allow 1 lb of sugar. Put the juice and sugar back into the pan. Wash the mint, dry it and tie loosely in a bunch. Add the prepared mint to the juice and sugar and, stirring until the sugar is dissolved, bring to the boil.

Boil briskly until setting point is reached. Take out the bunch of mint and add the finely chopped mint. Stir well, then pot and seal.

CRAB APPLE JELLY

Use the juice to make jelly, the pulp to make jam! You can use whatever amount of apple you like, just ensure that you have the right proportion of sugar to juice.

Crab apples
Water
Sugar

Wash the crab apples and remove the stalks. Cut the fruit up roughly, peel and core, and put into the pan. Add enough warm water to cover the bottom of the pan. Simmer over a low heat for about 10 minutes until the juices begin to run, then cook on a higher heat until the fruit is very soft and pulpy.

Pour the fruit into a scalded jelly bag and leave to drip. You can squeeze the last drops of juice from the bag, but be careful, for any pulp that comes through the bag will make the jelly cloudy.

Measure the liquid. For each pint you will need $\frac{3}{4}$ lb sugar. Return the juice to the pan and add the sugar, stirring well. Put on the heat, making sure that the sugar is dissolved before the mixture boils. Bring to the boil and boil moderately fast until setting point is reached.

Put the jelly into warm, dry jars, cover with waxed paper circles and seal. Leave the jelly until set and cold before storing it away.

Making jam from the pulp: put the pulp from the jelly bag into a large basin. Add a teacup of hot water and stir to loosen. Rub through a sieve to remove the apple cores.

Weigh the sieved pulp and for each pound you will need $\frac{1}{2}$ lb sugar. Put the pulp and the sugar in the pan and stir over a low heat until the sugar is dissolved, stirring all the time to prevent burning. Bring to the boil and boil until setting point is reached. Pot in small warm jars and seal.

GREEN TOMATO CHUTNEY

This recipe uses no sugar, but dates instead to make a sweet, rich chutney.

4 lb green tomatoes
1½ lb onions
2 cloves garlic
3 teaspoons salt
1½ lb dates
1 level teaspoon allspice
1 level teaspoon peppercorns
1 red chilli, optional
2 level teaspoons ground ginger
1¼ pints malt vinegar

Skin the tomatoes by putting them into a basin and covering them with boiling water. Leave for one minute, remove from the water and the skin should be easy to remove.

Slice the skinned tomatoes thinly. Peel and chop the onion. Finely mince the garlic.

Put the prepared tomatoes, onions and garlic into the preserving pan with the salt. Put on the lid and simmmer very gently over a low heat for 20 minutes. By this time the juices should have begun to run. Remove the lid, turn up the heat and cook a little faster for 1 hour. By this time the onion and tomato should be soft.

Pick over the dates, removing any fragments of stone. Wash, then cut them into small pieces. Add the prepared dates, allspice, peppercorns and chilli to the preserving pan.

Mix together the ginger and ¼ pint of the vinegar. Stir into the other ingredients. Cook very gently for 2 hours, stirring frequently and adding the remainder of the vinegar as it is needed. Pot and seal well.

RHUBARB CHUTNEY

4 lb rhubarb
⅓ oz allspice
⅓ oz peppercorns
1 lb onions
1 level tablespoon salt
2 cloves of garlic
⅓ lb stoned raisins or sultanas
⅓ lb brown sugar
1 level teaspoon ground ginger
½ pint vinegar

Wipe the rhubarb and cut up into 1-inch pieces.

Tie the allspice and the peppercorns loosely in a piece of fine muslin.

Chop the onions finely and mince the garlic.

Put the rhubarb, onion, salt and garlic into the pan. Put on the lid and cook slowly over a low heat. When the juices begin to run, take off the lid and add the sultanas, sugar, ginger and the bag of spices. Turn up the heat and add the vinegar. Bring to the boil and boil fast for 25 to 30 minutes. Pot and seal while hot.

Moist Carrot Date Cake, page 103

Chocolate Fudge Cakes, page 97

Nan's Orange Bread, page 95

Teacup Apple Sauce Cake, page 102

Mrs Guy's Wartime Barm Loaf,
page 106

Oatmeal Welsh Cakes, page 109

"All the makings of a merry party"
DE LUXE FAVOURITES
Caley's Crackers
Mackintosh's
Carnival
Mackintosh's
Everybody's Favourites

Bible Cake

½ lb. Judges Ch. 5: v 25
½ lb Jeremiah 6 : 20
1 tablespoon 1 Samuel 14 : 25
3 Jeremiah 17 : 11
½ lb 1 Samuel 30 : 12.
2 oz Nahum 3 : 12 (chopped.)
2 oz Numbers 17 : 8 (blanched and chopped)
1 lb 1 Kings 4 : 22
1 teaspoon Exodus 35 : 28
3 teaspoons baking powder
Judges 4 : 19 (to mix)
Royal icing

Set oven to 335°. Gas Mark 3
Cream Judges 5·25 and Jeremiah 6 : 20.
Beat 1 Samuel 14 : 25 with Jeremiah
17 : 11. Add to Judges and Jeremiah with
a little Kings. Mix remainder of Kings with
baking powder, Samuel 30 : 12, Nahum,
Numbers and Exodus. Fold the Kings mixture
into the Judges and Jeremiah with enough
Judges 4 : 19 to make soft, dropping consistancy.
Grease and line a large cake tin. Put in
the cake mixture, scooping out a hollow in
the centre. Bake in the oven for about 1½
hours or until cooked. Cool on a wire tray
and ice when cold.

"A real 'Ovaltine' Girl"

" My little girl, Betty, aged 2½ years, is a real 'Ovaltine' girl. She has had it regularly three or more times a day since I ceased to feed her myself. She is wonderfully healthy and robust, and always full of energy and good spirits. Her height and weight are above the average, and her resistance to colds and other ailments is excellent. I am certain her good physique, clear complexion and her health and vitality are largely due to the health-giving nourishment provided by 'Ovaltine.' "

'OVALTINE'

Prices in Great Britain and N. Ireland, 1/1, 1/10 and 3/3 per tin.

P803

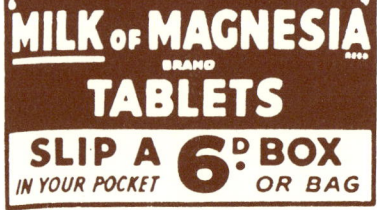